AUTHOR

Eduardo Manuel Gil Martínez (25 June 1970) is a historian and has been passionate about Spanish history for several years, mainly about the Second World War and the age of the Reconquista. Author of numerous texts on the Second World War for Spanish and Italian magazines such as 'Revista Española de Historia Militar', AMARTE, 'Ritterkreuz' or 'The Axis Forces in the Second World War 1939-1945'. In addition to the title we publish, he is also the author of: "Sevilla Reina y Mora. Historia del reino independiente sevillano. Siglo XI', 'Breslau 1945. El último bastión del Reich', 'The Spaniards in the SS and the Wehrmacht. 1944-45. The Ezquerra unit in the Battle of Berlin '", The Bulgarian Air Force in World War II. The forgotten ally of Germany', 'Romanian Armoured Forces in the Second World War', 'Hungarian Armoured Forces in the Second World War', 'Spanish Air Force in the Second World War', 'Hispano Aviación Ha-1112' (about the last Messerschmitt 109 ever built in Spain) and other texts for important publishers such as Almena , Kagero, Schiffer and Pen & Sword.

Juan Arráez Cerdá is a Spanish Aviation expert and owner of one of the best pictures' collections of Spanish Aviation. He is the author of many books and articles about Aviation (in French and Spanish).

PHOTO AKNOWLEDGEMENT:
LET: LUIS EUGENIO TOGORES
CCJ: CARLOS CABALLERO JURADO POR MEDIO DE JUAN ARRÁEZ CERDÁ
NEG: NEGREIRA POR MEDIO DE JUAN ARRÁEZ CERDÁ
BIBLIOTECA VIRTUAL DE DEFENSA (BVD)
JUAN ARRÁEZ CERDÁ (JAC).

PUBLISHING'S NOTES
None of unpublished images or text of our book may be reproduced in any format without the expressed written permission of Luca Cristini Editore (already Soldiershop.com) when not indicate as marked with license creative commons 3.0 or 4.0. Luca Cristini Editore has made every reasonable effort to locate, contact and acknowledge rights holders and to correctly apply terms and conditions to Content. Every effort has been made to trace the copyright of all the photographs. If there are unintentional omissions, please contact the publisher in writing at: info@soldiershop.com, who will correct all subsequent editions.
Our trademark: Luca Cristini Editore©, and the names of our series & brand: Soldiershop, Witness to war, Museum book, Bookmoon, Soldiers&Weapons, Battlefield, War in colour, Historical Biographies, Darwin's view, Fabula, Altrastoria, Italia Storica Ebook, Witness To History, Soldiers, Weapons & Uniforms, Storia etc. are herein © by Luca Cristini Editore.

LICENSES COMMONS
This book may utilize part of material marked with license creative commons 3.0 or 4.0 (CC BY 4.0), (CC BY-ND 4.0), (CC BY-SA 4.0) or (CC0 1.0). We give appropriate attribution credit and indicate if change were made in the acknowledgments field. Our WTW books series utilize only fonts licensed under the SIL Open Font License or other free use license.

For a complete list of Soldiershop titles please contact Luca Cristini Editore on our website: www.soldiershop.com or www.cristinieditore.com. E-mail: info@soldiershop.com

IN MEMORIAM: Eduardo Gil and Juan Arráez

Title: **SPANISH VOLUNTEERS IN GERMANY DURING WORLD WAR II - VOL. 2**
Code.: **WTW-059 EN** by Eduardo Manuel Gil Martínez and Juan Arráez Cerdá
ISBN code: 9791255891215 first edition May 2024
Language: English. Size: 177,8x254mm. Cover & Art Design: Luca S. Cristini

WITNESS TO WAR (SOLDIERSHOP) is a mark of Luca Cristini Editore, via Orio, 33/D - 24050 Zanica (BG) ITALY.

WITNESS TO WAR

SPANISH VOLUNTEERS IN GERMANY DURING WORLD WAR II - VOL. 2
WEHRMACHT, WAFFEN SS & SD

PHOTOS & IMAGES FROM WORLD WARTIME ARCHIVES

EDUARDO MANUEL GIL MARTÍNEZ
JUAN ARRÁEZ CERDÁ

BOOKS TO COLLECT

CONTENTS

THE BLUE LEGION (1943-1944)...5
    Formation...5
    Combat actions..7
    Repatriation..11
THE LAST OF THE LAST...35
    Spaniards within the Waffen SS, Wehrmacht and SD...................................36
    Fighting with the Wehrmacht, Waffen SS and SD...39
REPATRIATION...65
UNIFORMS..79
AWARDS..80
EQUIVALENCE OF WAFFEN SS AND WEHRMACHT RANKS WITH THOSE OF THE SPANISH ARMY...82
BIBLIOGRAPHY..96

▲ Various divisionaries pose for the camera during a moment of rest (NEG).

THE BLUE LEGION (1943-1945)

Due to pressure from the Allies, the Spanish government was forced on 24 September 1943 to withdraw the Blue Division (its last action of war was to repel a Soviet attack on 5 October 1943), but still leaving a small contingent of about 2269 men, in the so-called Blue Legion, to avoid setbacks on the part of the Germans in the repatriation of the Division. The latter began to take shape on October 20, 1943, and was officially constituted on November 17, 1943, at the level of a regiment and under the command of Colonel Antonio García Navarro. The repatriation of the members of the Blue Division was carried out in stages and was completed before the end of December 1943.

Formation

When the DA marched, there were about 2200 men still integrated into the structure of the German army, which was called the Spanish Legion of Volunteers (LEV) or more popularly known as the Blue Legion (in this text we will use the two ways of naming the Spanish unit interchangeably) and in Germany as the Spanische-Freiwilligen Legion, under the orders of Colonel Navarro. On November 17, General Esteban-Infantes signed the order that gave birth to the LEV. This Legion was incorporated into the German 121st Infanterie-Division and can be assimilated to a reinforced Infantry Regiment (in 1944 there were already many German Infantry Regiments that only had two Battalions, while the Blue Legion had 3 Banderas which corresponded to 3 Battalions). As a curious fact, the Spanish unit did not receive any identification number within the German Army.

A remarkable fact is that both the men of the DEV and those of the LEV always showed an affable character and an excellent relationship with the Soviet civilian population. In fact, not only did the Soviet authorities not bring charges of war crimes against the Spanish volunteers, but the Soviet civilians who lived with the Spanish troops were always very grateful for the humane behavior of the Spaniards despite the difficulties.

ORGANIGRAM

This Spanish unit was made up mostly of soldiers who had belonged to the Blue Division, and had approximately 2,269 volunteers (110 officers, 114 non-commissioned officers and 2,045 enlisted men) distributed in 2 Infantry Banderas, 1 mixed Health and HQ Bandera and the General Staff as follows (based on Caballero Jurado and Moreno Juliá):

Headquarters (Plana Mayor): Infantry Colonel with a degree in General Staff, Antonio García Navarro, last Chief of Staff of the Blue Division, with his second in command being Lieutenant Colonel Modesto Sáenz de Cabezón Capdet.

Staff, services and Gendarmerie: 174 men (of whom 78 belonged to the Gendarmerie). The General Staff was under the command of Commander Ramón Abenia Arenas and was divided into tactical HQ and administrative HQ; and the Gendarmerie had a Vanguard Section and a Rearguard Section.

First Grenadier Band: 579 men and the usual structure of a German infantry battalion.
Chief, Infantry Commander Antonio Ibarra Montis.
- Staff (with 59 men) which included an Assault Section.
- 1st Grenadier Company (with 122 men).
- 2nd Grenadier Company (with 122 men).
- 3rd Grenadier Company (with 115 men).
- 4th Machine Gun and Mortar Company (with 161 men, 12 machine guns and 6 mortars).

(Each company was composed of approximately three sections of 32 men, and a staff of 14 men, although this number of men was not exactly met).

Second Grenadier Band: 639 men and the usual structure of a German infantry battalion. Chief: Infantry Commander José María García Mendoza.
- Main Staff (with 75 men) which included an Assault Section.
- 5th Grenadier Company (with 138 men).
- 6th Grenadier Company (with 140 men).
- 7th Grenadier Company (with 135 men).
- 8th Machine Gun and Mortar Company (with 151 men, 12 machine guns and 6 mortars).

Third Mixed Band: 786 men and consisted of a mixed unit. Chief: Artillery Commander José Virgili Quintanilla.
- Plana Mayor (with 28 men).
- Anti-tank company (with 162 men). It consisted of 6 Sections that each had 1 50 mm cannon and 1 75 mm cannon. This company was the most motorized unit as it had 7 cars, 9 motorcycles and 19 trucks.
- Scout squadron (with 76 men). Made up of 2 Sections and a total of 6 light machine guns and 74 bicycles.
- Company of sappers (with 123 men). Made up of 2 Sections and a total of 6 light machine guns and 3 light flamethrowers.
- Transmission company (with 101 men). It consists of 1 radio section and 1 telephony section.
- Cannon Company (with 191 men). With four 75 mm cannons and 4 150 mm cannons.
- Legionary Squadron (with 44 men).
- Transport Section (with 25 men).
- Quartermaster Section (with 20 men).
- Military Police (with 21 men).
- Others (with 49 men).

Health (with 111 men).
It had 2 Sections, one for evacuations and the other for the Aid Post (which served as a Field Hospital).

Rearguard services (Riga): Evacuation hospital, paymaster's office, nursing home and interpreters. Also, in Königsberg and Berlin there were convalescent hospitals with Spanish staff (all with a small number of staff).

The 1st, 2nd, 3rd, 5th, 6th and 7th Companies were constituted as follows:
- Staff.
- 3 Rifle Sections (each Section consisted of 3 platoons). Equipped with a total of 9 light machine guns.
- 1 Mortar section (with 2 x 80 mm mortars).
- Combat baggage of the unit.

The 4th and 8th Machine Gun Companies were constituted as follows:
- Staff.
- 1 Tank Destroyer Platoon.
- 3 Heavy machine gun sections. With 12 machine guns in total)
- 1 Mixed mortar section. With 2 mortars of 80 mm and 6 of 120 mm.
- Combat baggage of the unit.

According to Caballero Jurado's study, each Bandera had 27 light machine guns, 12 heavy machine guns, 8 80 mm mortars and 6 120 mm mortars. As was the norm in the German Army, most units were hypomobiles, with each Bandera having only 1 truck, 1 car and 4 motorcycles with sidecars.

Combat actions

The Spanish Unit was concentrated at Jamburg (in the vicinity of Narva) in mid-November 1944. There the Blue Legion volunteers received (again) training and were re-equipped. As a curiosity, it should be noted that the facilities in which the men of the Blue Legion were quartered had previously belonged to the Red Army. In this brief but intense 3-week training period, the Spanish officers imposed strict discipline to better prepare the troops for their next combat intervention. On December 3, before completing the training, the Spanish troops had to participate in an anti-partisan operation called "Partisanschtshina" to dislodge groups of partisans near Krutyye Ruch'i. The units that had to carry out this mission were the I and II Rifle Companies of the I Bandera, a Machine Gun Section and the General Staff of the I Bandera. They left on the 1+3 in trucks in the direction of the village of Ivanovskoye, 5 km from Krutyye Ruch'i, with the mission of clearing the area of snipers and partisans, as well as to evacuate the civilian population (to prevent them from helping the Soviet guerrillas). Between the 3rd, 4th and 5th they were carrying out these "clean-up" missions and on the 6th they received the order to return to the Jamburg barracks, where between 16:00 and 16:30 the different Spanish units arrived by truck. The Spanish soldiers did not fulfill this mission with much enthusiasm because they had to evict civilians from their homes and later set them on fire, when what they wanted was to confront the Red Army. Despite this, they fulfilled their mission adequately, for which the Spanish soldiers were congratulated by the military commander of Jamburg.

The harshness was such that during this period of instruction there were 7 desertions and another 6 attempts and six self-mutilations were frustrated. Faced with this difficult situation, 75 men who were not considered "reliable" to remain in the Unit were forcibly repatriated to Spain.

The anxiety to fight was palpable in the air, but the Spaniards did not have to wait much longer, as they would soon be sent to Lyuban, and the LEV was added to the German 121st Division, attached to the XVIII Army and commanded by General Hellmuth Priess. The destination chosen to enter the line of the Spaniards was southeast of Leningrad in the area of Begogolovo-Shapki-Kostovo, an area where there were barely 4 or 5 hours of daylight a day. In addition, this area was west of the Volchow River and north of Lake Ilmen and Novgorod. As a swampy area, insects were plentiful and conditions in the middle of winter were very harsh. In addition to the swamps, there were forests of firs, high scrub, undulating terrain with frequent clearings, which made their precarious roads impassable; although from a defensive point of view it was an advantage since it made a major frontal attack against the Spanish units impossible.

On 13 December in Jamburg the Spanish unit was put on alert and the first to pick up the winter field clothes was the II Bandera. On the 15th at 6:00 a.m., the men of the II Bandera, already prepared for combat, left Jamburg in trucks to be transferred to the railway station, from where they departed at about 10:00 p.m. in a westerly direction towards Shapki. The men of the 1st Banner also received the order to leave on the same day 15 and headed by road to the railway station, departing at the same time as the 2nd Banner. The journey continued through the 16th, arriving at Shapki at 16.00. After disembarking from the train, the legionnaires walked 3 km on foot (the Unit's material was in trucks) to the vicinity of Kostovo, where they would stay in bunkers and uninhabited houses. The II Bandera arrived on the 16th at Shapki, leaving for Kostovo. On the 17th, the troops of the Third Bandera arrived in the third train, and the troops of the German 121st Division and the 405th Regiment were completely relieved. The area occupied by the Spaniards was 12 km from the static front line between Shapki-Belovo-Kostovo (a swampy and unhealthy area) where they relieved some German units from the front.

On the 18th at noon the First Bandera set out for the front line. To do this, he had to travel 26 km and immediately proceeded to relieve the two German units deployed there at about 5:00 in the morning of the 19th.

The 1st Bandera partially relieved the 2nd Battalion of the 407th Regiment, while the 2nd Banner partially relieved the 1st Battalion of the 405th Regiment and the 121st Alarm Battalion. South of the line of the Spanish troops was the 121st Battalion of Sappers and the II Battalion of the 405th Regiment; Ahead of the positions of the Blue Legion troops were swamps and behind them a series of roads leading to Kostovo. The final distribution of the troops was that on the northern front the 1st Bandera was deployed along 5 km and the 2nd Banner along the remaining 7 km, being flanked by the 407th German Regiment on the left and by the 405th German Regiment on the right. About 6 km from Kostovo was the "Westfalia" camp, which was where the command post of Colonel García Navarro was installed, as well as that of the III Bandera, the Company of Sappers (as a reserve of the Blue Legion) and two reserve sections of the I and II Banderas. For its part, the III Bandera was deployed in the rear in the towns of Belovo and Kostovo, leaving the artillery and anti-tank units distributed in these towns in order to support the front-line units. The 40-bed aid station was located in Kostovo, and a section for repairing cars belonging to the III Bandera was located in Shapki.

Opposite the Spaniards were the Soviet 177th Division and 614th Brigade. To the south was deployed the 80th Division and along the line were the 29th Artillery Group and the 12th and 124th Armoured Brigades and various rifle units. Despite all this Soviet potential deployed in front of the Spaniards, the area where the Spaniards were positioned can be considered as a well-chosen area by the Germans to avoid a frontal attack by the Soviets against a non-German unit. The Red Army was very calm, but that tranquility (only broken by the effect of typhus on the soldiers and by some small attacks that were adequately repulsed, although the Blue Legion suffered its first casualties) was the one that preceded the calm since in mid-January 1945 the "storm" would be unleashed on the entire German front that would end the siege of Leningrad forcing the Germans to retreat towards the Baltic States.

Specifically, on the same day, the 18th, at dawn, the Spaniards had to repel an attack by Soviet patrols, wounding a legionnaire of the Second Bandera, later another was wounded by mortar fire. On 18 December, the last train arrived with the remaining forces and supplies and they were stationed in Kostovo. Thus, between December 20 and 23, when the health and quartermaster services were definitively installed, the deployment of the LEV can be considered completed. Attacks by enemy patrols and consequent skirmishes with Soviet troops were frequent. In front of them, the Spaniards responded with mortar fire, keeping them in their positions.

Between 24 and 27 December, the Soviets made several attacks on the area where the Spaniards were, resisting enemy attacks well despite the harsh weather conditions. That tension that the Spaniards had was reflected on the 27th when a legionnaire who was the driver of the colonel of the LEV deserted. On 30 December another major enemy attack was repulsed. Already between January 11 and 12 the men of the Blue Legion are in a state of alarm, waiting for an imminent Soviet attack on the entire northern front.

Until 13 January, Soviet forces made few incursions into the "Spanish" zone, but harassment between the two sides was continuous.

On 13 and 14 January, the Soviets tested the Spanish and German positions on the flanks of the Spanish Unit. On January 14, 1944, the final Russian offensive began on the Leningrad and Volkhov fronts to liberate Leningrad. The German divisions in these areas were overwhelmed by the Soviet steamroller between the towns of Oranienbaum and Pushkin, although the Blue Legion did not receive the attack directly (although the German units deployed on its flanks did). During the night between the 14th and the 15th the Red Army began its winter offensive. The thrust of the Russian attack was such that the German lines were quickly shattered, and Novgorod was captured on the 20th. Faced with this situation, the general order was received to the entire XVIII Army to retreat along the Gatchina-Luga road. At first, the Spanish troops did not directly receive the Soviet attack, although the German units on their flanks were being attacked, so the risk of being encircled increased. On the 15th, the Soviets were still attacking the 408th Regiment. On the 17th, General Hellmuth Priess (commander of the German 121st Division) moved his headquarters to the area where the Soviets were entering and formed with the 407th Regiment and the LEV a combat group. On the 18th the Spaniards repulsed a Soviet attack, but as the situation was critical, the LEV Sapper Company (which was the Legion's reserve) received trucks to be transported immediately to the site where they were required.

In just 4 days the situation at the front was dramatic for the Germans, who were in retreat. The Spaniards, faced with the danger of being surrounded after the retreat of their German comrades, were ordered to retreat through a terrain full of forests and frozen rivers towards Lyuban. This locality was a key railway junction whose possession would allow the Russians to definitively break the German siege of Leningrad, so the Blue Legion was assigned to take the railway station.

On the 19th at 3:00 p.m., the order was received that from 00:00 a.m. the following day the positions of the Spaniards should be evacuated and retreat towards the Lyuban, in this locality the Spaniards would be responsible for defending the railway installations still in the hands of the Germans. The Spanish withdrawal from the Kostovo area was to conclude at 5:00 a.m. on the 20th, and orders were received to keep the withdrawal secret and to leave everything that could not be taken with them unusable. Both I and II Banderas retreated in the direction of Lyuban, albeit on a small scale, while III Bandera headed directly for Lyuban.

The withdrawal did not begin at the agreed time, but was delayed for several hours, with the first unit to withdraw being the II Bandera followed by the I Bandera. Although the Spanish troops took between 3-4 hours throughout the journey, the weather conditions due to the ice and snow, the poor condition of the roads they used and the narrowness of the route (because they could not pass through the narrow roads, three artillery pieces were blown up and destroyed made the retreat a very difficult task).

On the 21st a good part of the LEV had reached Lyuban, but it was not until the 22nd at 6:00 a.m. that most of the Spanish Unit could be considered completely regrouped. All the soldiers arrived exhausted due to the great effort made in this unexpected and rapid retreat. Just as the artillery pieces of the III Bandera arrived, they were placed on the outskirts of the town. Specifically, Section II with the 75 mm guns were deployed to the north of the village, while the III Section with the heavy 150 mm guns was deployed to the northeast of the village. For its part, the IV Section was deployed in the vicinity of the III Section with the intention of supporting any of the above; while the First Section with the 75 mm guns was left in reserve.

It would be January 23 when the last Spanish troops in retreat arrived in Lyuban, where the situation was chaotic with many abandoned vehicles, fires and destruction. But it didn't take long for the Soviets to appear, so together with German troops, a desperate and bloody defense of the city against the continuous attacks of Russian troops began. During this day, the unit that suffered the most casualties was the II Bandera, which bore the heaviest weight of the fighting, and after this the III Bandera. For its part, the I Bandera was left with the mission of defending the urban center of the perimeter of the town without actively participating in the fighting on this day. But the massive influx of Soviet soldiers seeping through the German defenses meant that the fighting did not take place on the outskirts of the town but also inside from January 23. The Second Banner was ordered to march to the Gladkiy marsh near Lyuban to relieve a German unit and establish flank liaison with other German battalions. At about 11:30 a.m. the 5th, 6th, and 7th Companies entered the front line and established their defensive line (the 8th Company remained in reserve along with the 2nd Bandera Staff at Il'inskiy Pogost). On the 24th, the troops of the 2nd Bandera had not yet managed to definitively establish their positions in the vicinity of the Gladkiy swamp and, although they did not find their German comrades, they did encounter Soviet troops camped on a nearby hill that began to attack them. The battle was immediate and bloody, wounding at least 19 Spaniards. Immediately it was reported that Soviet troops under the command of the 121st Division prepared an offensive action against the Soviets in which the Second Bandera was to cover the west bank of the swamp with its companies and establish a front a little further north (the Spanish troops would act as a retaining wall for the Soviets while German troops would carry out an attack in the direction of Ramtsy-Grustiuja). Colonel García Navarro decided to send the Exploration Company as reinforcement support. But in the meantime, the Soviets were getting closer and closer to Lyuban, cutting off access roads to the town. The Soviets were advancing rapidly with the intention of capturing the railway station, now defended by the Spanish. The Soviet siege with continuous attacks was answered by the Spanish with Spanish artillery batteries, as well as small counterattacks to keep the station open.

On the 25th, the men of the Second Banner, together with those of the Scouting Company, took part in numerous engagements against the Russian troops in the vicinity of the Gladkiy Marsh. On the 25th, Colonel García Navarro decided to replace the men of the Second Bandera with troops of the First Bandera.

During 26 January, numerous enemy patrols infiltrated through the defensive perimeter that both the Germans and Spaniards had at the Lyuban station. One of them managed to reach the railway station, but they were met by troops of the III Bandera and the enemy were repulsed. Although the Soviets had numerous casualties, the Spaniards also suffered casualties in addition to suffering the capture of some men. Around 8:00 in the morning, troops of the Second Banner arrived from the Gladkiy swamp, so once they were in the defensive belt of the city, they participated in the fighting. The 8th Company distinguished itself especially in numerous engagements, causing more than 60 casualties to Soviet troops and capturing enemy documentation. At 10:00 a.m., the cannon company received the order to retreat to the Luga road, while the II Bandera also received orders to withdraw. But only an hour later and due to the permanent Soviet attack on the population, the Second Bandera was again positioned in the front line to support the withdrawal of the First Bandera that was deployed in the forest near the village. Meanwhile, the 1st Company, which was on the front of the Gladkiy swamp, was also ordered to retreat to Lyuban.

It was necessary to keep the railway station open to allow the retreating German troops (thousands of men) to be quickly evacuated. Due to the fierce defense of the men of the Blue Legion, the Spanish Unit suffered heavy casualties. The withdrawal of the LEV from the front was motivated by German orders that the Blue Legion cease to belong to the 121st Infantry Division and remain at the disposal of the XVIII Army, for which it was to be transferred to Luga. The first unit to begin the retreat was the 1st Bandera, while the 2nd Bandera remained in the front line until the night of the 26th. For their part, the Germans had also decided to abandon the defense of Lyuban.

On the same day, the 26th, Colonel García Navarro received the Iron Cross first class from the general of the 121st Infantry Division, in homage to the LEV that in these battles for Lyuban in the face of the immense enemy superiority was able to avoid the encirclement of a large part of the German XVIII Army. In addition, General Georg Lindemann, commander of the same Army, congratulated the Spanish soldiers for having temporarily stopped the Russians in a key sector.

On the 27th the Spanish troops were relieved by units of the 407th Regiment in the front line and began the retreat. Although in principle they were going to be shipped by rail, Colonel García Navarro was informed that the railway line had been cut by the partisans so he ordered that the march had to be made on foot to try to reach Luga, the only way to access Luga was a secondary road that was very narrow (so much so that it allowed to circulate in one direction only) and surrounded by swamps.

At 2:00 p.m. on the 27th, the LEV began the march by its own means with all the material, preceded by German troops. From there the exhausted Spanish troops had to face 132 km of hardships as the Germans were unable to provide them with trucks for their transport.

The 27th ended and the Spaniards reached Apraksin Bor on the 27th of January, continuing their advance the next day without pause, practically sheltering in the wooded terrain against the harassment of partisan troops. At some points they received information from Soviet civilians warning them of the places where they should not pass or even of the presence of nearby partisan troops, this behavior was nothing more than the sign of their gratitude and friendship towards the Spanish troops (in memory of the Spanish Volunteer Division). On the 29th the retreat continued, with the pleasant surprise that the I Bandera for a short period of time was able to enjoy the transfer of its materials in German trucks. The harassment of enemy troops on the men of the III Bandera at Zaplot'e was quelled when the II Bandera arrived to support them.

After overcoming numerous difficulties, on the 30th the legionaries continued their retreat, suffering numerous attacks from partisan troops that did not prevent them from continuing their route to Luga. On the 31st, the first men of the I and II Banderas, the Sapper Company and the Scouting Company began to arrive in Luga. Little by little, the rest of the units and the III Bandera arrived.

The entire retreat from Lyuban had required a great effort on the part of the Spaniards, who after the bloody battles sustained defending the town, had to cover 132 kilometers in 6 days mostly on foot with bad weather conditions and the continuous harassment of the Soviet guerrillas who were fighting in the rear of the German Army until you reach Luga. The men arrived completely destroyed with their combat equipment and clothing completely deteriorated after so many days of marching and fighting.

On February 1, already in Luga, the state of Spanish unity was so deplorable that even the Germans asked not to use the city's defenses and to allow them to continue their journey to Estonia so that they could reorganize. Despite this order and general exhaustion, the morale of Spanish unity remained high. The German High Command did not consider it appropriate to risk using the LEV against the Soviet roller because of the risk that Spanish unity would be annihilated and the negative connotations they would create between Spain and Germany. Only a couple of days earlier, Colonel García Navarro had received orders to hand over all the material of the LEV, especially with regard to heavy weapons, vehicles and livestock.

After staying about 6 kilometers from Luga (in Luga-Jui) and handing over the rest of the weapons and impediments they carried, the soldiers of the LEV continued their journey to the German rear on February 4, being transported (now) by train through Estonia. The I and III Banderas did so from the Luga-Este railway station, while the II Bandera and the Compañía de Exploración (Exploration Company) did so from the Luga-Central station. They passed through towns such as Pleskau (day 7), Valga (day 8), Tartu and Taps (where they arrived on the 9th) after covering 475 kilometers. Once at Taps (a railway junction of great importance in the communication between Lenigrad and Tallinn), and marching on foot, the First Bandera went to Jäneda (where it was quartered) and the Second Bandera did the same, but in Pruuna. The rest of the LEV, which could not board the train due to lack of space, had to leave from Luga in a mobile column consisting of 3 trucks and 9 cars, which finally arrived at Taps on the 10th after having been slowed down by a Soviet attack on Pleskau.

Once Colonel García Navarro had all his men, the LEV was redeployed on the 10th as follows: I Bandera (Jäneda), II Bandera (Lehtse-Pruuna), III Bandera (Taps), Intendancy (Aegviidu) and Plana Mayor (Jäneda). Due to its non-combat-ready status, the LEV was included in the Front Reserve. The Spanish soldiers were again subjected to a period of training while the LEV was reorganized and properly armed with the idea of being able to use the Spanish unit again in the future (in fact, on 2 March an order was received to prepare the LEV to be deployed in defense of the coast of Narva), but as we will learn below, on March 16 the LEV was demobilized.

Repatriation

Evidently, Allied pressure forced Spain to definitively cut off its aid to Germany. On February 20, 1944, the Führer and Francisco Franco agreed to the repatriation of the Blue Legion (although Hitler had already decided even before unilaterally). The repatriation order will arrive at the Legionary Command Post on March 3. For the men of the LEV, knowing that they would be sent home to abandon the fight at such a critical moment for their German comrades only lowered the morale of the entire unit. In spite of this, and on the occasion of the German gratitude to the Spanish volunteers, farewell acts and ceremonies took place, with numerous senior officials of the German Army attending them.

And on the 6th of the same month at 11.34 a.m., in the town of Lechts, Colonel García Navarro made his last harangue to the legionaries:

"... The news is sad and impressive: Spain, according to the German government, is going through the painful, I could say tragic, trance of agreeing to our repatriation."

"Come back proud of having done your duty...! We are proud because Spain demanded it of us and because it has been carried out without hesitation"

"... Now an order. The harshest I've ever given to the Legion. No one will show joy! I know you don't have it, because I see tears in many and emotion in everyone. We cannot feel joyful, no matter how great the desire was to return to Spain, to reconnect with our natural affections, or because family misfortunes suffered or some abandoned interests required our presence.

No one will rejoice: Spain is in mourning and the Legion is in black. Black in the seriousness, in the feeling, in the bitterness of the return."

"... On this day of mourning, you will wear your rifles turned upside down, as in funerals or as in Holy Week, because, I repeat once again, it is a day of mourning for our whole country."

On the 14th, the LEV received the official farewell of the XVIII Army in the town of Pruna; Lindemann delivered a final harangue to the Spaniards and decorated several officers and soldiers.

On the 16th, the legionaries surrendered the weapons they carried, except for pistols and revolvers that would serve to defend them if necessary. On the same date, the first contingent of Spaniards departed by rail for Könisberg (currently Kaliningrad, belonging to the Russian Federation), where they would arrive 3 days later. There they will concentrate on the military installations (truppenübungsplatz) of Stablack Süd near Königsberg in East Prussia.

On March 21, the last weapons and part of the leftover wardrobe were delivered, changing their German uniform for the Spanish one. At this time the Legion can be considered dissolved the next day, although it would still take about two weeks for them to deliver their German uniforms in Wilmehoff, to receive the Spaniards themselves. The stipulated withdrawal of the Blue Legion was carried out in a practical way between March (the first train of soldiers arrived at the Spanish border on March 28 and on March 31 the first repatriates arrived in Irun) and April 1944 (on the 11th or 17th, depending on sources, the last men arrived, among which were their colonel and the Legion's General Staff); It takes about four days to travel from Königsberg to Irun. The repatriation began with the Third Mixed Bandera (the Transmission Unit started the march), followed by the First and Second Banderas; to finish with the Plana Mayor (HQ). All that remained was to return small groups who had been tasked with finalizing all the documentation, liquidating the surplus material and repatriating the Spaniards hospitalized in the hospitals of Königsberg and Riga.

Once the entire Blue Legion was in Spanish territory, it only took a few days for the Government of Madrid to officially announce the extinction of the Spanish Legion of Volunteers on April 30.

▲ Well-equipped Spanish ski soldiers (NEG).

▼ A Spanish soldier during one of his visits to Berlin during rest periods (JAC).

▲ Blue Division Cemetery in Grigorovo. Crosses of the division soldiers' graves lined up at the foot of an altar with a large cross. In the background, left, the hospital in Grigorovo (DP).

▼ Spanish Unity pledges allegiance to the Führer in his fight against communism (JAC).

▲ Emilio Esteban Infantes with his General Staff and Wehrmacht troops (JAC).

▼ Spanish soldiers during training (NEG).

▲ Spanish soldier with a pennant of the SEU (Spanish University Union), from which many volunteers came for the war against the Soviet Union (JAC).

▲ The DA kitchen was vital to the unit (NEG).

▼ DA members in Nuremberg during a visit (NEG).

▲ Spanish soldiers cross the Volkhov in a rubber dinghy (NEG).
▼ Some members of Blue Squadron in their Luftwaffe uniforms (NEG).

▲ The sound of the trumpet signalled the time of day for the men of the DA (NEG).

▲ Spanish soldiers generally did not show a strict adherence to the uniform, although in official photographs the uniform was respected (JAC).

▲ Speech by General Esteban Infantes at another moment of the LEV formation act and the march of the last divisionaries (LET).

▼ In this photograph, headed by Colonel García Navarro, one can see the heterogeneous uniformity of footwear, trousers, belts, wars and caps that could be seen in the German Armed Forces in the last years of the conflict (LET).

▲ Colonel García Navarro during a farewell ceremony to one of his decorated men (LET).

▲ The Spanish soldier, having seen his behaviour in combat (it is no coincidence that many DEV and LEV members were veterans of the Spanish Civil War), was always a welcome companion for the German soldier (LET).

▼ Colonel García Navarro, head of the LEV, with General Amado Loriga to his left. The latter played an important role in the recruitment of LEV members (LET).

▲ Three Legionnaires sharing cigarettes (LET).

▼ Famous photo of Spanish soldiers posing with 3 Flemish Legion comrades on an artillery piece (LET).

▲ LEV formation with the national flag flying in the air at Stablack-Süd (LET).
▼ Four LEV members pose in Spanish uniform with German insignia in the Stablack-Süd barracks (LET).

▲ Pruna image of the LEV General Staff.

▼ Colonel García Navarro looking on as he bids farewell to the LEV (LET).

▲ Colonel García Navarro in conversation with a staff officer in Pruna (LET).

▲Visit of a German delegation to the LEV headquarters accompanied by the head of the LEV (LET).

▼ Review of the three LEV flags in their Spanish uniforms by the Chief of the Königsberg Army Corps, General Wodrig. After the LEV's official farewell to the German Armed Forces, the story begins of a few hundred Spaniards who, even at the risk of losing their nationality, continue the war with Germany (LET).

▲ Another moment of the LEV farewell ceremony in Königsberg (LET).

▼ Despite its short existence, the LEV was able to maintain the DEV's legacy of courage, pride and dedication in the fight against the Soviets (LET).

▲ Colonel García Navarro in his emotional farewell to the LEV (LET).

▲ Another moment of the visit by García Navarro and General Lindemann (LET).

▲ With this act, the LEV ceases to belong to the units of the Wehrmacht (LET).

▼ Arrival of General Lindemann and Colonel García Navarro at the headquarters of the 121st German Infantry Division (LET).

▲ Shot of Colonel García Navarro informing his men of the repatriation of the LEV. "...The news is sad and impressive: Spain, in agreement with the German government, is going through the painful, if not tragic, process of approving our repatriation" (LET).

▲▼ Incorporation of the LA into the 121st Division. General Rpiess, commander of the 121st Division, gives an account of the LA.

▲ Enrique Fernández Adán, one of the Spanish soldiers of the Blue Legion (NEG).

THE LAST OF THE LAST

For various reasons, some Spaniards decided not to return to Spain despite the risk of losing their Spanish nationality if they collaborated with the German armed forces. These men, ex-divisionaries (ex-DEV) and ex-legionaries (ex-LEV) mainly, together with other men who crossed the Spanish border to join the German armed forces of their own accord and many Spanish civilians who worked in the interior of the Reich, who lost their jobs due to the incessant Allied bombing of factories and German industry in general; They decided to fight as part of the German troops.

After the withdrawal and dissolution of the Blue Legion (March 1944) the intervention of the Spaniards with the Axis was illegal, which did not prevent some volunteers from refusing to return to Spain and other Spaniards from crossing the border into France.

To many of the men who were ordered to retreat, the idea of having to abandon their comrades now that Germany's situation on the Eastern Front was beginning to complicate and the fighting was still unfinished, made no sense at all. This situation is what motivates many of them to think of staying to continue their struggle against Bolshevism, but again the strong pressure from the Allies made the Spanish government commit itself to consider as deserters any of the Spanish soldiers who did not return with the expeditionary contingent. Whenever texts are reviewed in this sense, we are led to the idea that the Royal Decree promulgated on July 24, 1889, which condemned to the loss of Spanish nationality any citizen who serves in a foreign army at war, unless the citizen in question has a special permit from the Head of State, was still in force during this period. Specifically, Article 25 of Title One of Book One of the Spanish Civil Code refers as follows (published by the Royal Decree of July 24, 1889):

1. Spaniards who are not Spaniards of origin will lose their nationality:

   a) When, for a period of three years, they use exclusively the nationality which they have declared to renounce when they acquired Spanish nationality.

   b) When they voluntarily enter the service of arms or hold political office in a foreign State against the express prohibition of the Government.

2. A final judgment declaring that the interested party has committed falsehood, concealment or fraud in the acquisition of Spanish nationality renders such acquisition null and void, although it shall not have any detrimental effects on third parties acting in good faith. The action for annulment must be brought by the Public Prosecutor's Office ex officio or by virtue of a complaint, within a period of fifteen years.

As we have seen, this article 25 is quite consistent with the general idea that the Spanish Government made stateless a good number of Spaniards who decided to continue in the struggle; but the drawback to believing this fact for sure is based on the title of this article which clearly states "Spaniards who are not Spaniards of origin will lose their nationality". So we can see that the article is not aimed at Spaniards who are of origin, or in other words, the vast majority of Spaniards.

In any case, the Spanish Government, possibly without admitting that all those who rendered military service to belligerent governments would lose their Spanish nationality, considered that support for the Axis powers was becoming less and less productive and it would be the most politically correct thing to avoid as far as possible the existence of Spanish military units in the conflict. This situation was reflected in the official declaration of the Government of Spain in January 1944, in which they expressed their opposition to Spaniards remaining incorporated into the different military branches existing in Germany.

This official declaration was intended to put an end to the clandestine crossing of the Spanish-French border by Spaniards who had been encouraged by the German secret services in Spain and by Falangist leaders to join the German Armed Forces.

However, according to Clyde Clark (taken from the GUTENBERG website), he comments that the Spanish legislation existing between December 21, 1943 and January 1, 1945 guaranteed amnesty to those recruited from other countries or deserters who remained abroad. (Clark, Evolution of the Franco Regime (n.p., 1951), 442, 555-56). Although we must refer to the regulations in force, which were those published by the Royal

Decree of July 24, 1889, as mentioned above, and which were possibly used incorrectly to obtain the purpose intended by the Government.

The government's objective is to put Spanish "volunteers" between a rock and a hard place; What a bitter decision is presented to all those whose intention is to remain at their posts in the face of the inexorable Soviet advance. This eventually leads to many of them eventually abandoning their idealism and "romanticism," and must return to reality. The war seems increasingly lost to the Axis, and Spain cannot maintain the policy that brought them closer to them about three years ago. But these vicissitudes are not going to prevent a good handful of these soldiers from persevering in their idealism and staying with the German troops.

Spaniards within the Waffen SS, Wehrmacht and SD

But it was not only some soldiers of the Blue Legion who remained in their fight against Communism since, from Spain, in the most pro-German circles, a fairly large number of men (mostly ex-combatants of the Blue Division), given the circumstances, considered returning to German territory to join them in a personal capacity.

Even before the Blue Legion was repatriated, in certain circles close to the Falange, the formation of a new unit of Spanish troops in the service of the Germans began to take shape. Recruitment must be as secret as possible, in order to avoid Francisco Franco's intention to stop all these activities; and it is carried out mainly in Spain itself at meetings of the Falange and in groups of veterans of the Blue Division. Already from the departure of the Legion to Spain, some men are "invited" by German officers to remain in the conflict on their side, enlisting in some units of the Wehrmacht.

Other "volunteers" come from unemployed or Spanish workers in the Reich who consider that the move to the army will be economically or socially beneficial to them. Some Spanish exiles (former republicans) will also be recruited who, after having served in labor battalions, have in some cases been forced to wear the German uniform. Although the latter would be few, they preferred to serve with other Spaniards rather than in the conditions in which they found themselves.

But the Spanish authorities are not going to make it easy, since the order has been given to "protect" the border crossings in the Pyrenees, in direct contact with occupied France. The Civil Guard (Guardia Civil) receives strict orders to prevent the passage of these men, with the instruction to shoot them if necessary. And although these orders were carried out to the letter, it is true that in some of the cases, these members of the Civil Guard could not help but feel a great dose of respect and pride from those men who risk their lives, their families and even their own nationality to cross a border that will take them back to the chaotic spectacle that is the last year of war that still remains for Germany until she is finally defeated. They are men who do not back down from the oath they took to fight Bolshevism, nor from the oath they took in many cases with their German comrades-in-arms: "I swear to God, that in the struggle against Bolshevism I will unconditionally obey the Captain-General of the Armed Forces, Adolf Hitler, and that as a faithful soldier I am willing, Anytime he may desire, to lay down my life for this oath."

Although many of them were shot or killed while trying to cross the border under fire from the border guards, others did manage to reach France. Where the Germans who knew the events that were happening in Spain in this sense, received these Spaniards with little less than open arms. To better organize them, the Germans established recruiting stations, where they would be documented and integrated into the German Armed Forces.

The existence of Spaniards in the Waffen SS was far from unknown, and an example of this are the two letters sent from the Spanish Embassy in Berlin to the Spanish Ministry of Foreign Affairs that deal with this matter: On May 11, 1944, the Spanish consul in Berlin sent the following letter to the Spanish Minister of Foreign Affairs: "It has been reported that many ex-combatants of the Blue Division are currently crossing the border of the Pyrenees clandestinely, they do so with the assurance that they will be well received by the German authorities... several of these ex-combatants have rushed to enlist in the Flemish SS Legion to return to fight on the Russian front." (A.M.A.E. File R-1079). In a letter dated July 6, 1944, the Spanish ambassador in Berlin informed the Spanish Minister of Foreign Affairs about the clandestine presence of Spaniards in the German armed forces. Many of these Spaniards display national emblems on their uniforms (referring to Spanish emblems) in addition to the insignia of the SS..." (A.M.A.E., File R. 1079).

The Spanish volunteer units of both the Heer and the Waffen SS were formed throughout 1944 and the first half of 1945 thanks to the enrolment of men from various backgrounds. Spanish workers working in Germany in the summer of 1944 were recruited here, mainly from two well-defined groups. Some came from the 50,000 who went to work in the Reich after the signing of the economic agreement signed between the Spanish and German governments in August 1941; others were Spanish emigrants in France, including both those who were emigrants before and after the Spanish Civil War (republicans who fled to France and who after the German invasion of the neighboring country had been recruited by the German authorities, especially for the Todt Organization). Although there would obviously be opinions of all tastes, it is obvious that many of the workers who joined the volunteer units did so more than out of ideology because of the possibility that these units gave them to leave the increasingly dangerous factories of the Reich, bombed day after day by the Allied forces. at the same time of the possibilities that could arise to desert at the most appropriate time if it were opportune, seeking to return to Spain.

The other large group that contributed men to these volunteer units are the aforementioned DEV and LEV veterans who chose to stay in Germany when they were discharged.

The recruiting units (belonging to Sonderstab "F") were under the direction of Dr. Edwin Maxel, who had been a member of the German liaison unit in the Blue Division and head of the Blue Division in the Blue Legion. He returned to Spain with the Legion, acting from the German embassy as recruitment coordinator, in direct contact with the SS BrigadeFührer Hansen ("El Batallón Fantasma" - Carlos Caballero). The origins of the Sonderstab F date back to 1941 when it was created under the command of D. Helmuth Felmy (whose initial of his surname gave the unit its name); although the relationship between the Sonderstab F and the Spaniards dates back to the beginning of 1944. The Sonderstab F, which operated from January 1944 to August of the same year in the south of France, had "offices" in the border regions near Andorra, Port Bou, Hendaye, Puigcerdá and with its headquarters located in the city of Lourdes. Once they had been registered at the headquarters of Sonderstab F, the new recruits were sent to a reception camp located in the Quartier de la Reine in Versailles ("Queen's Barracks"). There they were greeted by Luis García Valdajos, veteran of the Division and Blue Legion. He was at Versailles, stationed by the training center at Stablack Süd (in East Prussia), with the mission of coordinating and escorting the contingents of Spaniards to Stablack. After being subjected to the corresponding medical check-up, almost all those admitted were transferred to Stablack, while a few were recruited by the SD for a new unit created in February 1944, the Einsatzgruppe Pyrenären of Sonderstab F, destined for anti-partisan work through its infiltration of the Resistance. This mission was aided by the abundant presence of anti-fascist Spaniards in the maquis of the region. Among the Spaniards recruited by the SD there were also Republican exiles.

From at least June 1944, a group of Spaniards were quickly put into action serving in the Sicherheitsdienst (SD). Some of these soldiers had been Spanish Republicans exiled in France, who were eventually to serve as spies. Their missions were mainly carried out in southwestern France, although they are also named in actions against the French resistance and against the Allies in Normandy.

The Spanish embassy in Berlin estimated that by the summer of 1944, there were approximately 1500 Spaniards working for the German security services in French territory, although this figure was possibly "inflated". This led to official protests from the Spanish government, but German diplomacy claimed to be unaware of the facts, justifying them as isolated cases and confessing their inability to do anything about the matter.

The first group of Spaniards under the command of García Valdajos had to reach Stablack by 15 April at the camp. Once there, the men were again subjected to endless training and retraining, even though many of them had previously been combatants. To re-instruct men who in many cases were more trained than the average German army seemed absurd to them. But that's how the German organization worked, for better or worse.

The number of Spaniards welcomed in Versailles could reach the figure of 300 by May 1944 and a figure close to 400 in June, where after the pertinent classification they were sent to East Prussia being framed in the Freiwilligen Einheit Stablack (Stablack Volunteer Unit) under the command of Artillery Captain Wolfram Gräfe and Ensigns Loinant and Panther. There were also several non-commissioned officers, some Information and Propaganda officers and several female assistants (between 5 and 6). All of them were of German origin and for the most part had served in the Liaison Staff with the Division and the Legion.

It was intended that the entire staff of this Unit would consist of a Staff and three companies with three sections of grenadiers each (and each section with nine men); It was also considered necessary to set up two deposit companies (reserve and instruction).

In Stablack Süd, García Valdajos was recognized for his previous rank of lieutenant, after the first contingent of men arrived. Once the Spaniards were settled there, García Valdajos gradually acquired a role of administrative control in the training of the new recruits until June (the 6th), leaving Ezquerra to impart the purely military tasks. On 7 June he went to Paris for a course for SS-SD officers in the fight against the maquis, after which he would not return to the training centre.

An important fact to keep in mind is that in Stablack Süd, volunteers with employment would not be accepted, or in other words, that the jobs and decorations of those who had served in the Legion or Division would not be recognized, and that they should all serve as soldiers. It was also decided that Spanish soldiers would wear the uniform of the Wehrmacht, with the pay equal to that of German soldiers.

The Spaniards received the uniform of the Heer without any specific insignia of their nationality and took the oath of allegiance to Hitler. Later they received a complete equipment with a wide variety of weaponry; as well as a comprehensive instruction that included German classes.

At the end of April or beginning of May 1944, the Spanisches-Freiwilligen-Einheit (Spanish Volunteer Unit) was created in Stablack, with an initial strength of close to 250 men, composed as planned of a staff and three companies of grenadiers, in addition to the two depot companies.

The unit that the Spaniards stationed there began to call the Batallón Fantasma (Phantom Battalion), because of its "theoretical" non-existence since this was always a rumor among the Spaniards present in Germany and was never made public due to the opposition of the Franco government to Spaniards continuing to fight in the Wehrmacht.

All the men who had been "collected" by the Reich were heading to Stablack Süd, leaving the barracks of Versailles practically deserted of Spanish troops, as they were moving rapidly towards East Prussia. In this regard, a telegram from the Foreign Unit Command of the OKW dated 16 May 1944 reports the presence of a single Spaniard in the Versailles barracks, while 1 officer and 10 other men had left for Königsberg five days earlier. NARA T77/885/5634629.

At the beginning of June 1944, from Stablack the unit moved to the town of Stockerau and Hollabrun, near Vienna (the former about 15 kilometers from the capital and the latter 25 kilometers), where the entire unit was renamed Freiwilligen Einheit Stockerau. In the vicinity of Vienna, the reserve units (Freiwilligen Ersatzbataillon located in Hollabrun) and instruction units (Freiwilligen Ausbildungbataillon located in Stockerau) and its third company, still in the process of training with the volunteers who continued to arrive (despite their "non-existence" between June 8 and July 20 there were about one hundred and fifty). His first two companies, now completed, marched to the town of Solbad Hall im Tirol (this town retained that name between 1938 and 1974, now called Hall im Tirol), near Innsbruck, for training as mountain troops for eight weeks. The entire unit will be named Freiwilligen Einheit Solbad Hall. This training was directed and guarded at all times by officers who had been liaisons between the Blue Division and the Heer. The Spanish volunteers insisted to the Germans that they not be led by Spanish officers, perhaps because of their fear of the Franco regime, since officially the Spanish dictator had promised the Allies that no Spaniard would continue to fight for the Axis. As a result, as it grew, the unit had a mix of young Spanish and German officers, and even the former Blue Division officers who joined the unit did so as simple soldiers, having to earn promotion on their own merits. Once in Stockerau, the Spanish troops were commanded by the well-known German SS artillery captain Wolfram Gräfe, who had previously led the Unit at Stablack Süd.

So, what many Spaniards wanted, which was to serve together in an all-Spanish unity, did not happen. It was not really a propitious moment to do so in principle, since a proper Spanish unity would once again lead to increased pressure from the Allies on Spain with the consequent risk of the opening of a new front from the Iberian Peninsula. Despite this aspect, there were also those who did not wish to be part of any Unit that was led by Spaniards, as can be seen from a note from the Foreign Unit Command of the OKW dated May 10, 1944 where it reports the dispatch to Königsberg of 60 Spaniards recruited in France who had shown their desire to serve in the German Armed Forces under German command, better than into the Spanish Army. (T77/885/5634630).

Despite being a volunteer unit, some complaints soon arose, mainly referring to the cultural and disciplinary clash between Spaniards and Germans. As a result, about 50 men asked to be transferred to a Schutzkommando of the Todt organization in the south of France.

As for the total number of Spanish volunteers who fought with the Waffen SS and its security forces, it is completely impossible to establish an indisputable figure. But there is some consensus that after June 1944, the figure must have been around 1,000 Spaniards (Berlin Document Center microfilm, T354, A3343, U.S. National Archives).

In June 1944, when the two Spanish companies arrived at Solbad Hall, Tyrol, they acquired their official designation of 101st Spanische-Freiwilligen Kompanie and 102nd Spanische-Freiwilligen Kompanie, the first under the command of Lieutenant Panther and the second under the command of Ensign Leiffen.

The 101st Spanische-Freiwilligen Kompanie had four rifle platoons and one command platoon; There was no specific data about the 102nd, which was possibly similar, taking into account that a third company was in formation. In general, the designation of the entire Unit was Freiwillige Einheit Solbad Hall.

In this barracks, as mentioned above, the Spaniards were preferably instructed in specific exercises of mountain troops (which will determine in the future the areas to which they will be sent to fight) in addition to learning the handling of all types of weapons. The camp, close to the city, was situated on the hill of a wooded hill. An old building that functioned as a convent some time ago, will be the headquarters of the command of the companies that will be formed there.

During this period of instruction, the now "classic" clashes between Spaniards and Germans resurfaced, which would lead to the murder of a German soldier by a Spaniard surnamed Echevarría. Evidently, the fact that former Spanish commanders served as private soldiers did not help much to ensure that the Germans treated them properly.

The probable number of men that was "assembled" at Solbad im Hall Tirol was at least 200 for each of the two companies formed, with more men arriving in dribs and drabs. Since some of them had no training at all, they were transferred in some cases to the Todt Organization.

Fighting with the Wehrmacht, Waffen SS and SD

Upon completion of training in August 1944, soldiers were placed in German units as diverse as the 357th Infantry Division, the 3rd Gebirgs Division, or anti-partisan units of the 3rd Brandenburg Division Regiment. Another contingent of Spaniards served for the SD and about 50 men carried out anti-partisan tasks in the Pyrenees area until they were transferred to Otto Skorzeny's Jadgverbande.

The 101st Company attached to the 3. Gebirgs-Division (belonging to the XVII Armee Korps of the Wehrmacht's Army Group Ukraine South), departed on 16 August 1944 from Solbad im Hall Tyrol by train to Vienna from where they will take a course near Budapest. Before leaving Austrian territory, in Vienna, they are subjected to an air attack that they have to respond with the anti-aircraft machine guns provided for this purpose in the railway convoy. It will be the section under the command of Corporal Pérez Eizaguirre that, because it corresponds to him in his turn, will have to face the attackers, resulting in a wound. After passing the bombardment, the train continues its route to the Hungarian capital, Budapest. From here they leave for the also Hungarian Debrecen, but not before having to wait for a group of sappers to put the destroyed railway in parts back in good working order, after the air attacks also suffered on Hungarian territory. From there they finally departed for what would be their final destination, the Bukovina (region located in the north of Romania and Moldova, southwestern Ukraine and south of the Galicia) in mid-August 1944, under the command of Ensign Panther. The train stops at the Romanian station of Vatra-Dornei, belonging to the department of Cámpulong. The men of the 101st disembarked there and camped for two days in tents on the outskirts of the town. On the third day, Panther ordered the men to be formed and, after reviewing, they were directed to the positions of the 3rd. Gebirgs-Division about 70 kilometers away. This distance will be covered on foot by the Spaniards, and when they arrive, they will have as their main order to collaborate with the 3. Gebirgs-Division in keeping open the mountain passes through which the German troops retreat to the West under continuous pressure from the Soviets. The Spaniards went through their positions passing through towns such as Iacobeni, Valea Putnei or Pajorita, which placed them on their "new" operations front. They will finally reach their destination 48 hours after their departure from Vatra-Dornei, to join the 1st Battalion of the 3rd. Gebirgs-Division in Cámpulong (now Cîmpulung Moldovenesc), on the banks of the Moldova River. In just 11 days, our men have gone from safe Tyrol to the front line of a front line that threatens to crumble and be swept away by the unstoppable Soviet "red tide." Eventually the Spaniards were assigned to the 17th Company (ammunition carrier) of the Gebirs.Jäger-Regiment 138 (17./Geb.Jg.Rgt.138). With the collapse of the Wehrmacht's Army Group Ukraine South in the face of the powerful Soviet offensive, the 3. Gebirgs-Division fought for control of the mountain passes of the Eastern Carpathians, suffering significant casualties (according to data they were high, ranging from 57 to 70 dead, prisoners and missing). The tasks carried out by the Spaniards were aimed at slowing down the Soviet advance as much as possible by protecting the retreat of the German army; blowing up bridges, sabotaging railways and roads, establishing defensive posts at strategic points, etc. The Spaniards did not act with the whole company, but in small groups that allowed for more precise and silent handshakes. On 27 August, Romania switched sides following the coup d'état that deposed Marshal Antonescu, leaving the Axis troops in the Carpathians in an even more complicated situation having to force their painful retreat from their position about 3 kilometers from Cámpulong to rearward positions from 31 August due to the imminent danger of being trapped behind enemy lines. The men of the 101st were harassed by both regular Soviet troops and their former allies, the Romanians. As has been mentioned, there were many Spaniards who fell in these battles, since the orographic difficulties and the high number of enemy forces did not act in favor. It was the members of the 101st Company who covered the retreat of the last German forces over the Campulong bridge over the Moldova, causing the bridge to be blown up when the last troops passed, then they returned in a southwesterly direction in search of the well-known town of Vatra Dornei. A German motorized group closes off the motorcade of German troops fleeing to safer territories to the west, leaving logs and obstacles on the roads with the intention of slowing the rapid advance of the Soviets. The Spaniards begin to retrace their steps, leaving behind villages they passed through when they joined the battlefront; finally fortifying itself on a mountain called Muntii Sureanuluni, about 30 kilometers from the town of Cámpulong. The remnants of the battered Company are finally isolated in enemy territory, due both to the speed of the retreating German troops and to the imposing Soviet advance in the direction of Hungary seconded by the extra support obtained thanks to the attack of Romanian armed groups belonging mainly to the Romanian Communist Party, which will not cease to harass them. The feeling of abandonment is total and discouragement spreads among the 18 Spaniards who remain under the command of a German ensign whose name we do not know. As we mentioned, skirmishes follow one another day after day, although the rugged landscape abundant in giant pines and steep terrain plays in favor of the Spaniards. In spite of this, they suffered some casualties such as that of Ramón Pérez Eizaguirre who was captured when he left his position in one of the blocks defended by the Spaniards to go to look for food in nearby shepherds' huts (he would remain captive until 1954 when he returned definitively to Spain). He had already fulfilled the same task on other occasions to get milk, corn and other food, being wounded on one occasion by the Soviets, but "the pitcher went so far to the fountain" that on the 20th (or 15th?) In September, another encounter with the increasingly abundant Soviet patrols ended with his capture by them. The men of the 101st finally manage to leave behind the dangerous Romanian mountains to enter the no less dangerous Hungarian lands.

On October 13, during a Soviet offensive, at least 8 Spaniards were captured. There was nothing left to do but to continue the retreat and the direction followed by the small group of Spaniards would be at least relatively safe Austria, leaving behind the unoccupied lands of Hungary, where they would possibly manage to "couple" with a freight train that would take them to their destination as Vadillo reflects in his book "Los Irreductibles". Exhausted and shattered by nearly two months of continuous fighting and significant physical and moral exhaustion, possibly only a dozen Spaniards were the survivors who were able to join their compatriots at Stockerau and Hollabrunn at the end of October. The Spanish troops attached to the 3rd Gebirgs division received several citations, decorations and promotions due to their good work in the Carpathians.

Possibly a number of men totaling one company (the 102nd), were assigned to carry out anti-partisan tasks in Yugoslavia around the middle of August (possibly the 16th), establishing their headquarters in Celje (belonging to the municipality of Zalec) in present-day Slovenia (in German Sachsenfeld). The Spaniards commanded by Lieutenant Ortiz, although there are doubts as to which Unit they were attached, seems to be the most credible version that they were integrated into the 8th Company of the 2nd Battalion of the 3rd Regiment of the Brandenburg Division. This Unit became a Franco-Spanish company and was led by a Captain Stregner or Traege (according to Gerard LeMarec in "Les français sous le casque allemand" in the first case or according to Antonio Muñoz in "Forgotten Legions" in the second case). Apparently, this Unit would reach a total of

250 men, among which the Spaniards would be a minority since at least 180 would come from France. Some of these men remained in the north of Yugoslavia (with orders to fight Tito's partisans, although with few encounters with them), and another group extended their anti-partisan tasks into Italian territory led by Lieutenants Ortiz and Demetrio following the 7th Company which was of mostly Italian origin, where they acted at various points. They will face the Italian partisans in towns such as Bevagna, Perugia, Arsoli, Carsoli, Avezzano or Terni. Subsequently, they were located in the area of Arezzo and Citá di Castello; later they joined other "Brandenburgers" north of Turin in September 1944 (specifically in Ivrea), from where they retreated to the south of France, although as we will see some of the Spaniards were left behind and incorporated into the "Karstjäger". It was in that month when, as we will discuss in greater detail later, the Abwehr was "absorbed" and part of its troops were transferred to the Jadgverbänd Südwest.

At the end of October, as a result of the advance of the Soviet army and Tito's Yugoslav forces, the Spanish troops located in the north of Yugoslavia withdrew first to Hollabrunn and in December to Stockerau.

With respect to those who had deployed in northern Italy, during this retreat, some of the Spaniards were left behind, being absorbed by the 24th Waffen SS Gebirgs Division "Karstjäger" 59. Gebirgsjäger-Regiment of the 24th. Waffen-Gebirgs-(Karstjäger)-Division der SS of Sturmbannführer Werner Hahn. Here they would concentrate on a Spanish company with the designation 5. Kmp./II.Btl. (Spanish-Kmp.) belonging to the SS-Gebirs-Regiment 59, under the command of W-Ustuf. Jose Ortiz Fernandez. Other names of the members of this company are Trápaga (also W-Ustuf or according to Sourd in his book "Croisés d'un idéal" would hold the rank of oberscharführer), Antonio Pardo or Federico Martínez. (information taken from the Axis History Forum AHF). According to Ortiz's testimony, he took a course at Solbad Hall in Tirol to qualify as a Waffen-SS officer, after which he recruited Spaniards from factories and prison camps around Vienna. With these men he would increase the potential of his 5th Company of the 2nd Battalion, which he would command with the rank of untersturmführer. The section chiefs will be Trápaga and Unterscharführer Meleiro, Ozores, Millán and Solís; all former veteran sergeants of the Spanish Volunteer Division except Trápaga, who for medical reasons (also according to Sourd) could not join it.

From November 1944 onwards, the Karstjäger fought mainly in the Friuli-Venezia Giulia region (German: Julisch Venetien) in northeastern Italy and also in western Slovenia, as well as in Croatia with remarkable success. The Spanish Company would be fully operational with an approximate number of about 100 men (according to Sourd) between November and December, acting in anti-partisan tasks at Villach and Pontebba, and later at Tolmezzo. According to Sourd, in March 1945 they acted in the area of Trieste in the battle for the city of Gorizia (on the current border between Italy and Slovenia) against Tito's partisans. According to the testimony of a German veteran of the "Karstjäger", the Spanish company was very aggressive in the battles that took place mainly in the Chiaporano sector, in which the combat ended up being hand-to-hand. Many of those wounded in the fighting were taken to field hospitals in Udine and Gorizia; although its end was very tragic for the latter, since after the capture of Gorizia by the partisans, the wounded were massacred. Among these were at least 14 Spaniards from the "Karstjäger".

On 8 April (although according to Sourd there are other sources that place these events in March), the section commanded by Oberscharführer Trápaga, was surrounded at Ponte di Canale, suffering significant casualties. Quite possibly the rivals of the Spanish troops were Slovene partisans.

At the end of the war, the men of the "Karstjäger" also fought in the regions occupied by the British troops, even facing the famous desert rats within the framework of the 8th Army, becoming more and more involved in the commission of brutal excesses in their work and other senseless atrocities. Especially ferocious was the behaviour of the Italian members of the Division, as well as that of the Slovenes and Croats on operations in their homeland, further east.

On 28 April, the German troops in the area were ordered to retreat towards Austria, leaving the small Spanish unit in Pontebba with the mission of stopping the enemy advance and thus gaining time to allow the German withdrawal.

There is no reliable data to prove that any Spanish soldier participated in the retaliatory action taken by the Germans against the town of Avasinis on 2 May, although it cannot be ruled out either. At the beginning of May 1945, the Spanish volunteers were given permission to escape and try to reach Spain; however, the fighting against Tito's Yugoslav partisans in the interior of Trieste lasted until 5 May 1945, after the British troops (8th Army) had already occupied all this territory. as well as the city on May 2. At least 25 Spaniards belonging to the 5. Kmp./II.Btl. (Spanish-Kmp.) surrendered to British troops (6th Armoured Division) in the Rosen Valley. The men who remained in Yugoslavia withdrew in October to Austria. Fighting continued during the retreat to the Drau, as well as in the area of Slovenia that remained under German control until the last day of the war or Carinthia (Kärnten in German) in Austria until 10 May when they surrendered to American troops two days after the capitulation of the Reich (according to Sourd, the date of the final capitulation of these men would be the 9th).

Men of this 102nd company in Italy and Yugoslavia devoted themselves to plunder and rape, in addition to the many atrocities committed in the clashes with the Yugoslav partisans, mainly and to a lesser extent Italian. Of those who did not flee and were left behind, those who were luckier surrendered to the U.S. troops, ending up interned in concentration camps; But many of them were captured and killed by the partisans. Some tried to find their way out of the Spanish consulate in Venice; unsuccessfully due to the overwhelming pressure exerted against them by the new pro-communist Italian authorities. Others tried to do so via Milan, but they would also be discovered by communist partisans who would dash their hopes of returning to their homeland. Finally, some of them, such as Sergeant José María Ozores, did manage to flee, after going through numerous difficulties and dangers in northern Italy, and return to Spain.

The arrival of Spanish refugees was of such magnitude that in November 1945 (months after the end of the conflict in Europe) a couple of hundred Spaniards remained in Italy waiting to be repatriated by the Spanish embassy. Of these, most were veterans of the "Karstjäger" and to a lesser extent of other units (Sourd even cites the Ezquerra Unit) and some former workers in the Reich.

With regard to the Spaniards of the Brandenburg retreated to France, the General Staff of Army Group E, located in the South of France, attempted the formation of a company of Spanish legionnaires. According to Antonio Muñoz in "Forgotten Legions" on page 198, men of the 8th Kompanie II. Bataillon 3. Regiment "BR" which was where the Spaniards were framed, constituted the so-called "Streifkorps Biscaya" as part of the "Streifkorps Süd-Frankreich". These men, led by Lieutenant Demetrio from July 1944, were joined by some Spaniards from the Todt organization, constituting the so-called Einsatzgruppe Pyrenären, who fought the maquis in the south and southeast of France; totaling about 50 men (according to Sourd this Einsatzgruppe Pyrenären would have been constituted directly from the Sondestab F in January 1944, although this point is debatable since I do not have any other source to confirm it, the "Brandenburg" origin of this Unit being more credible).

The Einsatzgruppe Pyrenären, during its period of activity, distinguished itself in the anti-partisan struggle against the Maquis (very abundant mainly in the south-west of France). Since many of these maquis were former combatants of the Spanish Republic during the Spanish Civil War, these confrontations led to extreme aggression between them that led to the carrying out of various acts that could be described as "war crimes" by both sides.

During the existence of the Einsatzgruppe Pyrenären, it so happened that a couple of men in the SD were temporarily assigned to this Unit with the mission of "hunting" an important member of the OSS (American secret service) who had the Pyrenees as a field of operations in close collaboration with the French Resistance. One of these men was Rufino Luis García Valdajos, who had been stationed in Sonderstab F and who was "captured" by the SD, which he would enter with the rank of SD Obersturmführer. The other man was another Spaniard, a friend and companion of García Valdajos; his name was Ricardo Botet Moro. Botet Moro, like García Valdajos, had been captured in Stablack Süd by an SD officer, in this case it seems that his name would be Ellis or Ehlers (according to Sourd).

Returning to the search for the OSS agent in the Pyrenees, it seems that it was not very effective on the part of both men. This was due, according to them, to the fact that they were "abandoned" somewhere in the south-west of France with civilian clothes and a certain amount of money to manage themselves for a season in the search field; But they lacked accurate information on where, how and when to act to capture the American agent. The result was, as Botet recounted, "We didn't try to find anybody. We didn't fully understand the orders and we had no idea where to start the search" (in Sourd).

Miguel Ezquerra, who had been "attracted" by the SD, which he joined with the rank of SD Hauptsturmführer, also took part in various anti-guerrilla missions in the early summer of 1944 in the south of France.

The Spanish Einsatzgruppe Pyrenären Unit was to be constituted in Pamiers (in the French district of the department of Ariége), although when we found ourselves in the summer of 1944 after the Normandy landings, it was difficult to form the cadre of it, since there would be many who waited for the Allied occupation to "disappear". Together with the Streifkorps, Süd-Frankreich withdrew from France during the summer of 1944 in the face of advancing Allied forces.

In September 1944 (Sourd reports that, in June, although in the different sources consulted, it is more real and credible that it happened in September taking into account that it was in July of that year the attempt against Hitler that accelerated this process), when the process of absorption of the Abwehr took place, the Streifkorps Süd-Frankreich was transferred to the SS-Jagdvervänd Südwest, a formation under the command of Obersturmbannführer Otto Skorzeny.

The SS-Jagdvervänd Südwest had the strength of a small regiment, presenting the following organization (according to Sourd's data):
- Staff and Combat School
- SS Jadgeinsatz Italien (made up of Italian volunteers)
- SS Jadgeinsatz Nordfrankreich (constituted by French volunteers)
- SS Jadgeinsatz Südfrankreich (made up of French and Spanish volunteers)

The transfer of men belonging to the "Brandenburg" to the Skorzeny Unit was motivated by the change of task entrusted to the latter. Following the July 20, 1944, plot to kill Hitler, Canaris and other senior Abwehr officials, who controlled the Division, were linked to the events. Immediately control of the Division passed to the SD and it would subsequently become a conventional (though considered elite) fighting unit and as Infanterie-Division*Brandenburg* (mot) would be sent to the Eastern Front. About 1800 men from the "Brandenburg" managed to be transferred to the SS-Jagdverbände of the SS-Standartenführer obersturmbannführer Skorzeny, "tying up" to its special operations on the Western Front.

Possibly Demetrio's men attached to the Einsatzgruppe Pyrenären (and who knows if perhaps some of the men who had carried out "special operations" under the command of Miguel Ezquerra belonging to the Skorzeny Unit and who had acted in the Normandy sector) which according to Sourd would have been around 20-30 men, constituted the so-called "Kommando Kondor" attached to the SS-Jagdeinsatz Süd-Frankreich. They were assigned to a base near the Alsatian town of Molsheim, to combat the infiltration of French collaborators into the Liberated Areas. These Spaniards, according to Sourd, as well as their comrades of other nationalities, participated in various training courses in various sabotage tactics and special operations. These courses would take place in Tiefenthal and Wiesbaden between October and November 1944 (lasting three weeks) and another between January and March 1945 for further training (with a total duration of three or four days). From January 1945, the Spaniards of the "Kommando Kondor" joined the reconnaissance and sabotage missions in the rear of the American Seventh Army. In April 1945, the SS-Jagdvervänd Südwest was merged into the SS-Jagdvervänd Mitte; at the time, the latter was personally led by Skorzeny. It will be the remains of these troops who fought on the Western Front that in April 1945, after passing through the concentration center of Spanish troops in Potsdam in charge of Ezquerra, will be in charge of forming part of the defensive system of the Alpine fortress. Although the advanced nature of the conflict and the many difficulties of movement prevented them from ever arriving; So, they were disbanded in the last days of the war, fleeing to the Austrian mountains, preferably dressed in civilian clothes with the intention of taking advantage of the slightest opportunity to return to their homeland.

From October 1944, the remnants of the Spanish units that fought in Yugoslavia (102nd) were grouped in Stockerau and Hollabrunn with those that fought in the Carpathians (101st) and with the third Company that had been completed with the volunteers who had continued to arrive (the "remains" of Sonderstab F were transferred to Stockerau in the autumn of 1944). where he remained until the end of the war, carrying out his work as a recruit and organizer of the Spaniards who arrived).

Although the project to create a Spanish volunteer unit was still in force, at this time, the Spanisches-Freiwilligen-Einheit was incorporated into the Croatian depot brigade (Kroatisches-Ersatz-Brigade) which provided replacements for the German-Croatian divisions of the Wehrmacht 369th, 373rd and 392nd.

They formed the Freiwillige Ausbildungbataillon (Spanische), quartered in Stockerau, this unit would be under the command of the Ersatz Ausbildungsbrigade of the Croatian Volunteer Infantry Divisions of the Heer commanded by Colonel Klein; and the Depot battalion, the Freiwillige Ersatzbataillon (spanische), was stationed in Hollabrunn. This Croatian depot brigade provided replacements for the German-Croatian divisions of the Wehrmacht 369th, 373rd, and 392nd.

According to Georg Tessin, it was on 30 January 1945 that the Spanish volunteer companies 101st and 102nd, Freiwilligen-infantry-kompanien (spanischen), were created in Stockerau with the personnel of the reserve and training companies of the Spanisches-Freiwilligen-Einheit, which was dissolved. These companies were attached to the 357. Infanterie-Division. This theory seems to have no basis in reality since, as we have mentioned, the existence of the 101st and 102nd Spanish companies is already being discussed in Hall im Tirol.

A note from the archive of the Command of the Foreigners Unit of the OKW dated 16 December 1944 reports the dismantling of the Spanish Company into Army Group South, as well as the Spanish Training Battalion including the liaison personnel who previously served in the Spanish Legion in addition to the Spanish Volunteer Replacement Battalion in the XVII Military District centralized in Vienna. All these personnel will be absorbed by the SS. NARA T77/885/5634561 (U.S. National Archives and Records Administration).

The situation of "waiting" of the Spanish troops stationed in Stockerau, allowed that from the early date of December 11 to 17, 1944, the "abandonment" of the Austrian barracks of 33 men destined for the 28th SS-Freiwilligen-Panzergrenadier-Division "Wallonien" was registered. Although we will elaborate more on this transfer of men later. Faced with this situation, the commander of the Croatian Unit expressed his strongest protest against this "recruitment" carried out on men under his jurisdiction by the Waffen SS Unit commanding its Military District in Vienna on December 19, 1944. He also confiscated the travel permit obtained through the Waffen SS from a man named Rafael Barrio Toquero (he had served in the anti-tank unit of the 269th Regiment of the DEV and later in the Legion) who apparently was one of those who intended to join the Walloons (GUTTENBERG).

As has been shown in the file of the Command of the Foreigners Unit of the OKW dated December 16, 1944, in principle the departure to the SS units of the Spaniards had official backing, although it is quite possible that this was not the procedure for passing to SS units that could have been considered in the Command of the Foreigners Unit of the OKW. In spite of this, and as we will see below, this "official" transfer of the Spaniards to the Waffen SS will be stopped, being the new Unit of destination of the Spaniards the 357th Infantry Division, which did not belong to the Waffen SS.

On 25 January 1945, the 17th Military District (Vienna) established the 101st and 102nd Spanish Volunteer Companies as reinforcements for the 357th Infantry Division after disbanding the Volunteer Training and Replacement Battalions at Stockerau and Hollabrunn. The companies were suitably arranged with German liaison personnel (two officers, 44 men and six translators for each company) who possibly predominated among the Spaniards and moved to Sared (near Bratislava, known in German as Pressburg) where the Unit was located. Untrained personnel were assigned as labor for the work units. (NARA T79/94/672-3). These men served in the 357th until the end of March 1945.

This would have been the fate of the remnants of both companies, although everything changed due to the transfer at the beginning of February 1945, of some of these men to the 28th SS-Freiwilligen-Panzergrenadier-Division "Wallonien" following their "escaped" comrades in the same direction in the middle of the previous month.

Continuing with the events that had taken place in Stockerau since November 1944, it is evident that those who did not "desert" to the "Wallonien" and stayed with the German-Croatian Brigade became dependent on the 357th Infantry Division in September 1944 and ended up deployed in Slovakia, to the east of Bratislava, specifically between the towns of Levice and Neutra (Nitra in German). Those of the 101st will be the first to leave to join their new Unit, arriving after their transit by train, in the vicinity of a town that could be called Vajka (although it could well be another name, as F. Vadillo recognizes), on the banks of the Hron River, a tributary of the Danube. The members of the Spanish 102nd Company departed later, on 6 February from Stockerau, although after an air attack by the US air force, it was finally on the 10th when the train departed again, passing through present-day Bratislava on the 11th, after leaving Vienna behind, and stopping again in Leoben on the 12th and 13th to Nitra. Following their route, they reach Vrable, in the vicinity of the Zitava River, on the 14th. Finally, the men of the 102nd reach their destination on the 16th, as they will be "landed" in the small town of Kisgyekduyer, a few kilometers from their post in the German second defensive line; in which they will only remain for two days, since after these 48 hours, they are sent to the front line of fire.

Men from both the 101st and 102nd Spanish Companies were incorporated into the different units of the 357th, which by mid-January had been withdrawn from the front to resupply, the town of Neutra being chosen, in view of the forceful "hit" that the troops of the 2nd Ukrainian Front under the command of Marshal Malinovski showed; and in the case of the Spaniards with the Soviet 6th Armored Army belonging to that 2nd Ukrainian

Front. Already in January they confronted the Soviets at Nagy Kalna, about 50 kilometers north of the Hron (Gran in German). In February they took part in the counter-attack against the Hron bridgehead under the command of the I.SS-Panzerkorps. By the end of March, it was known that the Spaniards had participated in the Battle of the Hron River, where they would also suffer severe casualties. During this period the men were part of the Eighth Army, participating in the German defensive line that ran precisely along the Hron River in southern Czechoslovakia between 31 January and 2 March. From Fernando Vadillo we know of about thirty men from the 102nd Spanish Company, who, as mentioned above, were on March 8 in the vicinity of Kisgyekduyer, near the town of Vráble. From their positions they watched the course of the river Hron and until the 23rd they managed to hold their positions; as Kurt Jentsch (the leader of the small Spanish group, who also served as interpreter) was ordered to retreat to the second line. After two days, we located the group in Uibarch where they will have to face a powerful Soviet attack together with the Germans stationed there. After resisting stoically, they received a new order in which they were entrusted with the mission of clearing of enemies and then defending from them, a road along which German forces with mountain batteries were to retreat. From then on, the permanent retreat began, exposed at any moment to a Soviet attack or from the increasingly hardened partisans.

The new flight in formation will take the group of Spaniards to towns such as Topol'cany, Bánkovce, Trencín and later Nove Mesto na Váhom (in German Neustadt), where they will arrive on the last day of March. They then continue through Myjava (on the current border between the Czech Republic and Slovakia) where they arrive on 2 April, to reach Stráznice on 4 April and the Belusa railway station the following day. There they are miraculously accepted to board a train that will take them to Hollabrun, where they arrive around April 6. But they will not be in the Austrian barracks for long, as they receive the new order to board the next day a train that via Pilsen will take them to the German town of Hof on the 11th. In the barracks where they are picked up, they will spend a week resting from all their previous vicissitudes, after which they changed their uniform for civilian clothes and received the mandatory discharge from the German armed forces; at the same time, they were provided with documentation proving that they were workers hired by the Reich Government, which would later prevent accusations against these men who had voluntarily helped them to the end.

But returning to the situation in which the 357th Infantry Division found itself in March 1945, during which it fought bloody battles, the depleted Division had no choice but to retreat fighting in the direction of Bratislava and Vienna. About 40 kilometers back from Neutra, the 357th again took up new defensive positions under the operational control of the Panzerkorps "Feldherrnhalle" commanded by General der Panzertruppe Kleemann. Again, they were overwhelmed by the Soviets, heading northwest, specifically towards the area of Brno (Moravia). At the beginning of May, the remnants of the "shattered" 357th retreated again, pushed by the Soviet roller, in the direction of the towns of Iglau (Jihlava in Czech) and Deutsch-Brod (Havlikcuv-Brod in Czech), where they finally surrendered to their "pursuers". Only a few men, dispersed and separated from the bulk of the Unit, managed to break the encirclement by heading to Büdweis (Ceské Budejovice in Czech), to surrender to the Americans. Although some succeeded, they found themselves back in the hands of the Soviets, being handed over to them by the Americans and transferred along with the rest of those captured from their Unit, to the Soviet camps of Schachty, Kharkov, Stalino and even Moscow.

It is practically impossible for us to know for sure what happened to these men who fought in the 357th, although it is quite possible that most of the Spanish volunteers fell dead and very few were taken prisoner by the Soviets. Within this group we find the case of Corporal Jorge Mayoral Mora (born in Don Benito), a veteran of the DEV and the LEV, belonging to the Spanish 102nd Company and finally attached to the 357th, who was captured by the Soviets on March 20, 1945 in the fighting near the Hron River, when he commanded a platoon of Spanish volunteers. Also (according to F. Vadillo) Manuel Báez Gil (from Cádiz), Miguel Climent Sebastián (from Alicante), Manuel Rodríguez Martín (from the Canary Islands), Jesús Corral Martín (from Santander), Benjamín Vázquez García (from Galicia) and Juan Martínez García (from Murcia) also fell into the hands of the Soviets that same day.

Returning to the subject of those who "deserted" from the 357th Infantry Division, the fact of the transfer of troops to the Walloon division was motivated by the mediation of Antonio Alfonso Van Horembeke, a Belgian nationalized Spaniard, who had participated in the Civil War and who was at that time assigned to the provincial delegation of FET-JONS of Vizcaya. He was ordered to go to Germany at the end of March 1944 with the mission of gathering as many Spaniards as he could locate and enlisting them in the Flemish legion of the Waffen-SS. In this first "batch" of Spaniards recruited for the "Wallonien" were several non-commissioned officers with considerable experience in combat with both the Spanish Division and the Spanish Legion on the Eastern Front. Among them were Zabala, Ocañas, Cabrera, Vadilio and Pinar who immediately regained their former ranks, lost up to that point. Subsequently, another group of Spaniards arrived from Stockerau and Hellabrun through Beltrán de Guevara (an old friend of Horembeke who had joined the "Wallonien" in the first contingent from the Croatian Depot Brigade) who would go to the town of Hemmendorf, which was where the location of the "Wallonien" Depot was located at that time.

In July, after several months without having succeeded in his purpose, he will continue with his same task, although this time the Unit of destination will be the "Wallonien". He met a Walloon non-commissioned officer named Paul Kehren (also a veteran of the Tercio) in Poland at the end of September, and with him, they made contact with Leon Degrelle to propose the integration of Spaniards into the ranks of the 28th SS-Freiwilligen-Panzergrenadier-Division "Wallonien". Degrelle, always in need of new reinforcements for his dwindling troops, considered it a unique opportunity, so he accepted the idea and entrusted this mission to Van Horembeke. The latter came into contact with the SS-Ostuf. (First Lieutenant) Luis García Valdajos, because of his knowledge of the state of the Spaniards in the German armed forces. In September or early October 1944 an interview took place at the Hotel Adlon in Berlin between García Valdajos, Botet Moro (acting as interpreter) and Leon Degrelle, which definitely served to convince the Spaniard to join the "Wallonie", which took place on November 1st. García Valdajos, Kehren and Van Horembeke will begin their recruitment tasks in all the places where they could locate Spaniards to enlist from November to December. Evidently an important camp where they acted to recruit men were the camps of Stockerau and Hollabrunn, where, as mentioned above, several Spaniards "deserted" to the Walloon division. Another important "source" of Spaniards was those who worked in factories or even in other units of the Wehrmacht. It is difficult to say exactly how many men joined the Belgians from both camps, but it is certain that between them and those recruited in other areas it was possible to constitute an almost independent unit commanded exclusively by Spaniards and commanded by García Valdajos. At the end of November 1944, the first contingent of Spanish volunteers was concentrated in the camp that the Walloon division had in Breslau. The final number of Spaniards who joined the "Wallonie" could have amounted to a long hundred according to some, although more possibly it reached 240-350 men in January 1945 (this figure is approximate as can be understood, there are various opinions on the subject; thus Sourd says that there were about 350, Caballero Jurado puts the figure between 350 and 400; and according to the testimony of Albert Steiver it would be about 240). While the Spanish formation was being "composed", Botet Moro was sent to the SS Panzergrenadierschule Kienschlag located in Prosetschnitz (in the Czech Republic), from where he would return according to Sourd with the rank of Standaten Oberjunker. In the Walloon Unit, the struggle against the common Soviet enemy made it possible to strengthen the bonds of union between Spaniards and Walloons. The Belgian SS-Sturmbannführer Franz Hellebaut, recorded that these were integrated into the only battalion of the 70th SS Infantry Regiment of the division under the command of SS-Hstuf (Captain) Robert Denie, leading to the formation of a third company in the same (3rd Company of the first and only battalion of the 70th. Grenadiere-Regiment (3/I/70). SS-Ustuf was chosen as liaison officer with the rest of the division. (Ensign) Rudi Bal, who spoke Spanish because he had lived in Argentina years before. The Walloon and Spanish troops left Breslau and were first stationed in Olderhof (in the vicinity of Hanover) and were later sent to the Rhineland area, where they were prepared for a possible intervention in the Ardennes offensive, in which they did not finally intervene, although on December 24, 1944 a group of Spaniards under the command of the SS-Oscha (ensign) Ricardo Botet was in the area of Marmagen (Nettersheim) integrated into the After leaving the Western Front, they will move on in February to Stettin (now Szczecin) and the Stargard sector (now Stargard Szczeciński).

Although the leader of the Spaniards was, as mentioned, García Valdajos, Bal would become the effective head of the company when García Valdajos at the end of January 1945 remained in the Remagen area; Berlin being the next place where we hear of him again, at the beginning of the formation of the Ezquerra Unit when the troops of the "Wallonie" were sent to the front. This decision was mainly motivated by the fact that García Valdajos had excellent qualities in organizational and administrative tasks, his forte not being the command of the troops in combat. Still in the final phases of the training and before entering combat, another "transfer" of men from one unit to another took place, so that a group of about 30 Italian volunteers (the figure proposed by Sourd would be 50, although it is the only one of those consulted in which such a high figure is reached), composed of Italian workers in Germany and Italian emigrants living in Belgium, obtained permission to join the 29th Waffen Grenadier Division der SS (Italienische Nr 1)", mainly made up of Italians. Along with the Italians, there are about ten or twenty Spaniards who may have preferred to move to another area of the conflict closer to Spain. This small group of Spaniards was commanded by SS-Oscha Camargo and SS-Uscha Martínez Alberich, who were to be integrated into the Italian division by commanding a section of the SS-Regiment 81 of the 29th Waffen Grenadier Division der SS "(Italienische Nr 1)". This small group of Spaniards from the "Wallonien" were characterized upon arrival by wearing the winter camouflage uniform of the Waffen SS, which differed quite a bit from those worn by the men of the Italian unit. Their missions were mainly carried out to curb the increasingly frequent and emboldened partisan activities; only at the end of the conflict did they clash with regular American troops with acceptable results given the circumstances in the last days of the conflict in Europe. They may have taken part in fighting in the vicinity of Trieste and Brenner, although there is no confirmed information about this. In January 1945 they reached the Rodengo-Saiano area, where the Italian Division's training base was located. As an epilogue, remember that most of the men who surrendered from this unit to the partisans were immediately executed.

From mid-January 1945, the hitherto relatively inactive Soviets carried out a strong offensive that broke the Vistula Front. It takes only a few weeks for them to reach the Oder River, which leads to the German forces having to retreat and rebuild their defenses again. In order to establish a secure defensive front, new troops are called to the front line on the eastern front; among them is the Walloon unit (magnificently studied by Norling).

On 27 January, the "Wallonien" together with the also of Belgian origin 27.SS-Freiwilligen-Grenadier-Division "Langemarck", received the order to go to the front, without being very clear to which specific point of the front they would be detached. On January 28 they "boarded" several trains that would take them after leaving the western region of the Reich behind, to Stargard, where most of the men of the "Wallonien" arrived on February 6. Not all of them arrived as the General Staff Company and the 1st Battalion of the SS-Freiwilligen-Grenadier-Regiment 69 did not do so, due to the mistake of the Deutsche Reichsbahn (German Reich Railway) which disembarked them in Stettin (today Szczecin).

Returning to the Spaniards of the 28th SS-Freiwilligen-Panzergrenadier-Division, in the first days of February 1945, when the "Wallonien" was already deployed in the Stargard area (near Stettin) it received several expeditions of Spaniards from Vienna and Berlin. With these volunteers, the 3rd Company was completed to three sections and a fourth section was created in the 1st Company of the same battalion (an independent section that would be added to the V Cia of the Walloon SS-Ustuf Albert Steiver). These last reinforcements most likely came from the 101st and 102nd companies, as well as the occasional worker recruited at the last minute; some of whom, lacking adequate military training, preferred to be returned to their place of origin. Steiver himself, in his memoirs entitled "Krussow -1945 Wallons et espagnols", testifies to the actions of the Spaniards stationed there.

In the absence of SS-Hstuf Denie, Steiver assumed command of the battalion, as well as the mission of making the incorporation of the new Spaniards as useful as possible, who immediately had to face a long march of about 35 kilometers to reach their position at the front. According to Steiver's text, he estimated that there were about 260 men who arrived, although the number was possibly somewhat smaller.

The commanders of each of the three sections that made up the Company were SS-Oscha La Fuente (according to Sourd his rank would be Waffen-Hauptscharführer der SS) and Lorenzo Ocañas (according to Sourd his rank would be Waffen-Oberscharführer der SS), acting commander of the company being SS-Oscha Ricardo Botet (according to Sourd his rank would be Standarten Oberjunker) who combined this task with that of head of the 1st Section. Other names that formed as officers and sub-officers in the Company were Pedro Zabala, Juan Pinar, Cabrejas and the aforementioned Van Hoorembeke who had returned to "active" service after his activity as a recruiter for the "Wallonien".

The fourth section that was formed with the Spaniards who arrived, as mentioned, were added as a support unit to Steiver's 1st Company, with which it would participate in the battle of Stargard. This section came under the command of Sergeant Abel Ardoos (perhaps it was really Ardoz, his rank according to Sourd being that of Waffen-Hauptscharführer der SS) and they were quite well equipped, as they received heavy machine guns and anti-tank weapons, as well as a field kitchen. The fact that the head of this section was in Ardoos was a very positive account of his knowledge of both French and German.

In the vicinity of Stargard, Sourd relates, some Spaniards had a disagreement with a German officer belonging to an unknown Army Unit and his men. This disagreement was caused by the immediate trial to which three Polish women had been subjected after being accused of stealing potatoes from German warehouses; with the result that after being arrested they were sentenced to death. As chance would have it, the Belgian Hauptführer Denie and the Spaniard Botet Moro, together with another group of Spaniards, whose names we do not have, arrived at the farm where the sentence was to be carried out and were firmly opposed to its being carried out. Finally, after a great discussion in which threats were made on both sides, the Spaniards and Denie managed to free the women, although not without receiving a final threat from the German officer that would consist of no more and no less than a War Council. Shortly afterwards, during the march of the Spaniards to new positions, Sourd comments that five of them separated from the column in formation and supposedly were able to end the life of the German officer and some of his men to avoid their revenge for the events that had occurred.

Returning to the general disposition of the men of the "Wallonien", they are deployed in a sector of the front in which they coincide with a multitude of men belonging to the most diverse nationalities, and are integrated into the German defensive framework. There they will fight to stop the powerful Soviet "roller", from Norwegians, Swedes, Danes, Flemish, Walloons, Dutch, French, Estonians, Latvians to Spaniards; all in complete camaraderie fighting for a common goal. The Soviets were approaching south-west of Stargard and the arrival of the two Belgian units, both the Flemish and the Walloon, was urgently required. The area entrusted to the Walloons for defense is located south of the city of Stargard, leaving as a reserve force the only Battalion of the 2nd Regiment, which is where the Spaniards were integrated to form their 3rd Company.

It will be the Soviet 2nd Armoured Army and 61st Army Corps that will face the Walloon Unit. On February 7, the battle for Arnswalde, about 30 kilometers south of Stargard, reaches its climax. On February 10, Soviet forces rekindled their offensive against the city of Stargard; while the Spaniards made several incursions into territory occupied by the Soviets, demonstrating in each of them, great courage and fierceness in their actions. On the 11th, the 1st Company of the 1st Battalion of the SS-Freiwilligen-Grenadier-Regiment 69, temporarily attached to the 10th SS-Panzer-Division "Frundsberg", tried to conquer the village of Klutzow supported by some of the increasingly difficult to obtain air and armored units, as well as a good handful of men, including some Spaniards. The attack stalled, leaving the Walloons and the Spaniards in charge of defending that sector of Krüssow-Stardgard (currently Kluczewo-Stargard Szczeciński belonging to Poland), after the departure of the air and ground support they had for the offensive. Inevitably, Krüssow fell into Soviet hands, which led to the retreat of the Walloons to Wittichow (now called Witkowo) and Schneidersfelde (now Radziszewo) on 13 February. The 3rd Company, the Spanish Company, together with Rooryck's 6th Company and Lecoq's 1st Company, took up positions south of the town of Streesen (today the Polish town of Strzyżno).

On February 16, 1945, Operation "Sonnenwende" (Solstice) began, involving the SS divisions "Frundsberg", "Nordland", "Langemarck", SS Polizei, "Nederland" and "Wallonien", all under the joint command of SS-Obergruppenführer Felix Steiner. The "raison d'être" of this operation was to take advantage of the fact that the Soviets, after the important advances they had made after their offensive of January 1945 in which they went from the Vistula to the Oder, had exposed their flanks. In order to take advantage of this situation, the Germans would have to make an offensive "pincer" movement to encircle these troops and be able to overwhelm them. One of the "pincers" would be from Pomerania and the other from Hungary. But the cruel reality of the state of the German Armed Forces would prevent the obtaining of the necessary troops to achieve this, so the main objective of the German offensive would be to make contact with the besieged troops in Arsnwalde (currently Choszczno), a fact that was achieved on February 18, although at the cost of large and irreparable casualties without ultimately managing to "stabilize" the front line.

The main direction of the attack will be carried by the "Nordland" carrying as battering ram the 11th Abteilung Panzer "Hermann von Salza" and on both sides the 2 regiments of the division, the "Norge" to the east and the "Denmark" to the west. The men of the "Langemark" and the "Wallonien" covered the western flank; the "Frundsberg" and "Polizei" are in the direction of the Oder River; while the eastern flank was covered by the Dutch of the "Nederland" and by the "Führer Grenadier division". The 19th and 20th witnessed heavy fighting in the vicinity of Arnswalde, with the withdrawal of all forces south of the Inha River beginning on the 21st. The subsequent reorganization of the forces that are still "standing" in that sector, led the "Wallonien" to be subordinated to the control of the more powerful "Nordland".

On February 27, the Soviets advance with the intention of encircling the troops located in Stargard; kicking off the Battle for Stargard. In it, the Walloon troops are stationed in the vicinity of Kollin (present-day Kolin), about 15 kilometers from the town that gives its name to the clash. The casualties were again heavy, so much so that the only Battalion of the SS-Freiwilligen-Grenadier-Regiment 70 (also called 3/I/70), where the Spaniards were placed, had to be disbanded and its troops distributed among the two battalions of the SS-Freiwilligen-Grenadier-Regiment 69. Here the Spaniards, twinned with the Walloons, destroyed the Soviet tanks, mainly the well-known T 34, with their new anti-tank weapons (the dreaded panzerfaust), slowing down their advance as much as possible. It is known that during a clash the Spaniards armed with the panzerfaust attacked a group of T 34s, destroying one, damaging another one and making the group retreat. The patrols which the Spaniards will have to carry out will wear down more and more the already diminished forces that remained on a fighting footing; for these, showing their temerity, were sometimes surprised by the deadly responses of their opponents who were always on the lookout for the movements of the Spaniards. During this period Steiver's 1st Company and thus the Ardoos section were temporarily assigned to the "Frundsberg" Division.

On 3 March, the remnants of the defunct 1st Battalion of the division's 70th SS Infantry Regiment cover the "Wallonie's" retreat along the Baltic coast.

On 4 March, Stargard was definitively abandoned, with the Walloons and the Spaniards of Ardoos being the last to retreat, as well as the last to cover the civilian population trying to flee to the west and the military units that were in disarray looking for the rear lines. There have been 28 days of almost continuous fighting that have definitively depleted the section of the Spaniards who served in Steiver's 1st Company. These casualties could have reached up to 90% of its components in this section, although there is no precise data that can confirm the veracity of this information, it does give us a very approximate idea of the significant wear and tear of the section. The rest of the Spaniards integrated into the 3rd Company also suffered significant casualties, so much so that, as mentioned, they had to be placed in the SS-Freiwilligen-Grenadier-Regiment 69. Only about 60 Spaniards managed to escape the siege of Stargard in Pomerania at the beginning of March 1945, Rudi Bal, the then head of the Spanish company would fall in combat on March 6 at the head of his men, leaving it under the command of Pedro Zabala and Ricardo Botet.

The survivors of Stargard will be regrouped at Scheune, south of Sttetin, where they were originally part of a defensive line north of Berlin.

They were there for a short time, as orders were immediately received for all the Spaniards who were in the Walloon division to concentrate in the surroundings of Potsdam, an event that took place towards the beginning of March taking advantage of the fact that the units of the III German SS Corps were withdrawing in the direction of the capital of the Reich.

Possibly some of the Spaniards did not retreat to Potsdam and continued until the end of the conflict with the Walloon Unit, dispersed among their companies. Leon Degrelle himself, in an interview given in 1969 to the Madrid newspaper "Arriba", said that he sent Spaniards until the end of the war; which is possibly true, although we have not been able to confirm it with any document or specific information from the time.

Among the men who, after leaving the "Wallonien", were marching to Potsdam was Ricardo Botet and when they arrived at their destination, they were integrated into a new unit that, under the command of Ezquerra, was being developed in that place with Spaniards who had arrived from one place or another. Ricardo Botet put this on record in this statement:

"We received the order to go to Potsdam where all the Spaniards were being regrouped into a single unit, captained by Miguel Ezquerra Sánchez, it was bad for us to abandon the comrades of the SS-»Wallonie" with whom we had fought and shed our blood for the same ideal. When we arrived in Potsdam we were accommodated in a school for military orphans and there we found a huge circus show, there were more sergeants than soldiers, quarrelsome legionnaires, people of bad living, clueless people who did not know where to go and former veterans of the Blue Division and other units of the Wehrmacht, we would be approximately between 100 and 150. I remember among all of them a legionnaire who was Ezquerra's escort, had his face completely tattooed and wore a huge belt of the Tercio (Legión Española) with two pistols, one on each side. Years later, I was told that he died buried in the ruins of Berlin".

It will therefore be in Potsdam that the Ezquerra Unit will be born, which will defend the center of the capital of the Reich in union with an amalgam of defenders of multiple nationalities against the Russian roller that is already looming at the gates of the city.

Ezquerra, after his convalescence from the wounds suffered in the Battle of the Bulge, and García Valdajos, were entrusted with the mission of gathering as many Spaniards as possible, removing them from the various military units in which they might be placed, recruiting the Spanish workers in the industries of the Reich. or, in general, any Spaniard living in the Reich who met certain physical aptitudes and age. In this case, to facilitate the creation of this new Spanish unit, the help of General Faupel played an important role.

The unit created is completely heterogeneous, since in its ranks there is a mixture of former legionnaires (veterans of the African wars), veterans of the Spanish Civil War, the Blue Division and the Blue Legion; former "Wallonie" division, as well as workers who, having been working in the Reich, were now unable to continue their work in the destroyed German industries; Spanish members of the Todt Organization, Falangists recruited from Madrid, and Spaniards who, for various reasons, were imprisoned in German prisons.

Miguel Ezquerra therefore received orders from the German high command to track down the Spaniards likely to be enrolled in his combat unit in various German cities and towns. In this sense, he came to have certain tensions with the Spanish embassy, since the latter, as far as it could, tried to repatriate the Spaniards who were still in the Reich, without encouraging the creation of the Unit of Spanish combatants in the SS to be even far from the mind of Mr. Rodríguez del Castillo (the last representative of the Spanish embassy in Berlin).

In fact (as Vadillo recounts), in mid-April, between the 12th and 16th, Gonzalo Rodríguez del Castillo managed to evacuate some 200 workers of Spanish origin by rail. Since the 14th, the Spanish Embassy in Berlin has been without electricity (like so many other buildings in the battered city) and Rodríguez de Castillo moves his functions to the building on Berlinstrasse owned by the Falange. It was from there that he made his last calls to evacuate all the Hispanics who were in Greater Berlin; To this end, both radio announcements and Embassy notes in newspapers were used for this purpose. But the situation became extreme in the capital of the Reich and shortly after, on the 19th, it would have to be the Spanish diplomatic corps with Rodríguez del Castillo, who had to flee at full speed from there. On the same day, a small caravan of six cars and a motorcycle with a pennant and the license plate of the Diplomatic Corps leaves the capital, taking one of the magnificent highways of the Reich Road network, heading west, and then heading northwest, towards Hamburg. Throughout their journey they will mix with thousands of militaries and civilians going to one place or another (both fleeing from the Soviets and marching to meet them) and will be subjected to countless roadblocks by the Police, Army, SS or other security forces. Their "legal" status to try to escape the hell that much of Germany has become, thanks to their documentation, allows them to keep moving forward. Although the hardship of the journey will also take its toll on two of the vehicles of the Spanish caravan, which will be abandoned to their fate during the journey. When the Spaniards passed through the town of Wusterhausen on April 24, they were informed by German security forces of the presence of Russian troops only about 20 kilometers from the highway on which they traveled, where they had taken the town of Neuruppin. They speed up as soon as they could, since their capture by the Soviets, despite belonging to the Diplomatic Corps, would have an uncertain outcome and almost certainly deadly. In two days, on April 26, they meet in the city of Lübeck; From there they will "jump" to Hamburg and after two days there, they will head to what will be their final destination: Copenhagen. After the German surrender and when it came into force in the occupied Danish territory on 5 May, there were days of uncertainty in the Spaniards led by Rodríguez del Castillo, which ended when in the middle of summer (24 July), through the mediation of the troops of the United Kingdom, they were loaded onto an RAF plane to take them to London where their difficult and dangerous escape from a Reich ended German that crumbled minute by minute.

Going back in time again, to March 1945, we find that it will be close to the capital, the town of Potsdam, where the Unit of Spaniards that will go down in history as the Ezquerra Unit will be born; although its first chief was Obersturmführer Luis García Valdajos, who, as has been mentioned, was always chosen for organizational tasks due to his extensive experience in this regard, in addition to those he possessed for combat. So, he was the one who proposed Miguel Ezquerra Sánchez, who also had extensive experience as a front-line officer.

At the beginning of April 1945, the unit that Ezquerra had managed to recruit was roughly distributed as follows: It was based on the survivors of the 3/I/70 of the "Wallonie" and some men from other units in which a Spaniard had managed to "escape" (many of them had belonged to the Blue Division or the Blue Legion), as well as on students, workers of the Todt Organization or some outlawed by the German justice. In the end, the Einheit Ezquerra (some authors cite it as Einsatzgruppe Ezquerra) was composed of two companies that were quartered in Potsdam and in which the last volunteers were gathered.

Vadillo in his book "Los Irreductibles", mentions that Unterscharführer Ramón Baillo Fernández was sent by Miguel Ezquerra from Berlin to recruit Spanish volunteers from the Unit commanded by José Ortiz (already mentioned above), to the town of Tolmazzo, near Udine. As we can see, no effort was spared in being able to set up this last unit of Spaniards, which in a short time would go into combat.

Ezquerra cites in his book that some survivors of the SS divisions

Belgian and French were integrated into his Unit. But the reality is that there is no information in the existing documentation of both the French and Walloon units that this fact is true. It was possible that at some point during the Berlin battles some loose men from these Units temporarily ended up under the "jurisdiction" of the Spanish Unit.

To locate this recruitment and training center for Spanish troops in Potsdam, the German high command offered as accommodation an old school for military orphans, which had been an officers' school. And it will be there that they will be provided with weapons, which will be mainly light; although this supply of weapons will end when they arrive in Berlin, where they will be permanently re-equipped.

The days there passed with the completion of a light instruction on the men, in theory more dedicated to those who had not been in active military service in recent times, as was the case with the ex-workers of the Reich industries. The prevailing atmosphere, despite the complexity of the situation, was one of expectation and desire to start fighting against the Soviets. Not surprisingly they were volunteers, although it is also true that some were more convinced of their reasons for being there than others. Despite the voluntary nature of the Unit, it is possible that some men deserted during these days of training, as well as during the Battle of Berlin itself. Thus, although there are not very reliable data, it may be that in total there were half a hundred deserters.

This new company, a direct descendant of the 101, is once again referred to as such in various studies and in others as the Ezquerra Unit. These remnants of the 101st Ezquerra dependents were definitively integrated into the 11th SS Freiwillingen Panzergrenadian Division "Nordland", when the front was already in the vicinity of Berlin.

At the end of the fighting, some volunteers managed to escape from the German capital, while others were captured by the Soviets, some of whom would possibly be executed among the ruins of the German capital. The last Spanish prisoners in the USSR returned to Spain in 1954.

In addition to the Spaniards mentioned in SS formations, there are also reports of the existence of a few Hispanics in other units under the double rune. This is the SS Polizei Freiwilligen Bataillon Bozen, where it is said that they formed between 20-31 Spaniards and the 1st Company of the Dirlewanger Brigade with about 6 Spaniards.

As Sourd points out, in an internal document of the SS Sonder Bataillon "Dirlewanger" dated April 14, 1944, the names of 6 Spaniards are recorded. It is known that at least one of them, surnamed Rodríguez, had been transferred to the Unit from the SS Command in Prague. Another document dated April 15, 1944 presents us with the "Dirlewanger" incorporated into the SS Kampfgruppe Anhalt to take part in Operation "Frühlingfest" in Belarus under the command of SS Obersturmbannführer Günther Anhalt. In this combat group in which, according to Sourd, six Spaniards participated, in addition to the "Dirlewanger" there were also the SS Polizei Regiment 2 and 24, as well as other "minor" units. Little else is known about the Spaniards of this Unit (of penitentiary origin, since in its troops there were dangerous criminals and criminals from the prisons and concentration camps of the Third Reich), although it is assumed that they would continue in it until the end of the conflict (those who survived evidently, although there is no data on this matter) being able to participate in the repression of the uprising that took place in Warsaw, where this Unit did not exactly cover itself with glory, since it was guilty of numerous barbarities and atrocities with the Polish population and even with its German comrades from other units who tried to prevent their outrages. In favor of this is the information provided by Sourd in his book "Croisés d'un ideal"; since it refers to the testimony of a veteran of the Spanish Volunteer Division named Jorge Oriente, who had known a Spanish veteran of the "Dirlewanger" whose name he did not remember. The latter told him about his journey in German lands (after having served in the Spanish Volunteer Division) to which he arrived after crossing the French-Spanish border clandestinely, he ended up in Stablack where just with a dozen other Spaniards sent there, his previous ranks were not recognized. The discontent of this group led them to be court-martialed with the result of being sent to a disciplinary unit, which would be none other than the "Dirlewanger". In this unit, individuals of different origins were mixed, both Waffen SS, the Heer or even civilians imprisoned for various crimes. All the Spaniards (at least one of them had a police record, a very frequent occurrence among the members of this unit, so it is possible that the other 5 had some kind of crime on their record, although there is no proof of this) remained in the same section and participated in anti-partisan actions in Belarus (it would almost certainly be the aforementioned "Frühlingfest" operation). which would take place between May and June 1944. The anonymous veteran also told Jorge Oriente that they participated in the fighting that took place to put down the popular uprising in Warsaw in August 1944. After that, and already in full retreat against the Soviet "roller", they reached Slovak lands. There he contacted the Spanish consulate and finally managed to obtain false documentation as a Spanish worker with which he managed to reach Spain. Along with this veteran of the "Dirlewanger", at least three other Spaniards who served in that unit managed to return to Spain a few years after the end of the world war in Europe.

With regard to the men integrated into the "Bozen", the untruthful hypothesis about the Spaniards integrated into the police unit would be based on a "diffuse" origin of the origin of the Spaniards, who could have come from "stragglers" of a Spanish unit (the Blue Legion is mentioned) or on the other hand they could have come from the men of the police force.24 Waffen Gebirgs Division "Karstjäger". Since both the 1 Btl./SS-Pol.Rgt. "Bozen" coincided at the end of April 1945 in the same area of deployment as the "Karstjäger", the area of Tarvisio (in German Tarvis, located in the province of Udine in the Friuli-Venezia Giulia region). Of the approximately 100 men who would have been in the mountain unit, some 20 or 31 could have been authorized to join the Polizei, being stationed in Italy until the end of the war in the fight against the partisans. There is documentary evidence that shows us the list of 6 Spanish volunteers who died in northern Italy while serving in the SS Polizei Regiment "Bozen" possibly during March and April 1945. According to the German archives of the WAST (German War Graves Office) at least 3 of them would still rest in the cemetery of Costermano. According to Sourd in his book "Croisés d'un ideal", there is a document dated May 11, 1945, which mentions the existence of 25 Spaniards belonging to the SS Polizei Freiwilligen Bataillon Bozen (apparently after the German capitulation in northern Italy on May 2, these men escaped from the town of Bozen trying to avoid capture). While it is true that the previous units were most of the Spaniards under the flags of the Third Reich, there are also references (Sourd) to Spaniards in the Kriegsmarine (Naval Depot 28 in Sennheim), in naval coastal artillery units in Estonia, the Todt Organization, the NSKK, the "Speer" Legion or even in an artillery regiment of the 17th Luftwaffenfelddivision during the summer of 1944 on the Normandy coast (although it is It is true that there are no known documents about the latter and in Antonio Muñoz's book, "Göring's Grenadiers", there is no reference to the existence of these Spaniards; although it could well be some Spaniards who individually were incorporated into that Unit).

There must also have been several men with dual nationality (Spanish and German) who, being considered as volksdeutschen, could have been in any other German formation. A certain Frederick Lux, who served in the "Nordland" Division, is reported to have died on the Narva front (Narwa in German). According to Gonzalez, it is also believed that it is feasible that a Spaniard belonging to the "Wallonien" when the Walloon unit withdrew in the face of the Soviet push, ended up within the area of location of the 10th. SS-Panzer Division "Frundsberg" and join that unit. Only the name of one Spaniard who ended up joining the "Frundsberg" is known, Enrique Vázquez Mallo.

The transition from the Wehrmacht to the SS was not automatic or even specifically organized in advance. For it was the events that made the Spaniards who were trained in Stablack Süd within the Wehrmacht end up in many cases within the Waffen SS. It has already been mentioned that among the vicissitudes suffered by the 102nd, some of the Spaniards who formed part of its cadre were transferred to the 24th Waffen SS Gebirgs Division "Karstjäger" in October 1944; but the final step occurred when many of the Spaniards encamped at Stockerau and Hollabrunn "self-transferred" to the 28th SS Freiwilligen Panzer-Grenadier Division "Wallonien". There is no record that the numerals 101 or 102 were retained when they were integrated into the Walloon unit. For this reason, there is no proof of the existence of the sometimes mentioned 101 Spanische-Freiwilligen Kompanie der SS or the 102nd Spanische-Freiwilligen Kompanie der SS. It was when the Ezquerra Unit was formed that at least two companies of men were formed, who were nominally attached to the "Nordland"; and these two companies were able to recover the denomination that they already bore in Hall Tyrol of 101st and 102nd companies, but in this case belonging to the SS, although there is no reliable evidence to confirm this either, so it would be only speculation about the matter.

As a final assessment of the existence since 1944 of Spaniards in various German units, consider that neither the number of men, nor their dispersion, nor of course the situation of the war and the giant steps towards the defeat of the German Reich, made their general contribution in the Second World War especially significant. Let us remember that it is very difficult to establish a figure that really represents the number of Spanish volunteers who, after the departure of the Division and later the Spanish Legion of volunteers, were integrated into the Waffen SS, its security forces, the Wehrmacht and other formations; although this could well be around 1000 men, as recorded in the Berlin Document Center microfilm. T354, A3343, U.S. National Archives.

Leaving behind the number of volunteers, and bearing in mind the Spanish point of view and regardless of political connotations, we can value it as a worthy and heroic contribution in many cases to the annals of Spanish military history. They knew how to believe, fight and die in many cases, leaving the flag of their country high. Just as there were also Spaniards on the side of the Western Allies or the Soviets who also fought for their ideals, it is fair to recognize that these men deserve a prominent place (despite the small number of men we are talking about) in the Spanish military history of the twentieth century.

Now we will remind the combat actions of Spanish soldiers during the Battle of Berlin (the forementioned Ezquerra´s Unit that was based at Potsdam). The events we are recounting cover the period from 20 April to 2 May 1945, and in them we have abundant information about our men, except for the period between 22 and 26 April, which correspond to the first days of the Spanish presence within the Berlin defensive framework.

Friday 20 April:

After being stationed in Potsdam, not far from the barracks of the 9th Infantry Regiment, the Spaniards moved to Berlin by order of Obergruppenführer Gottlob Berger, head of recruitment for the Waffen SS.

The soldiers were informed of the orders received, leaving it up to each of them to make the personal decision to carry out this mission. They all volunteered, with no further doubts, except when and how they would make their move to the capital. They were thus volunteers among volunteers, for the most part, with extensive combat experience.

The group of Spaniards amounted to about 2-3 companies (more likely 2 than 3, the latter perhaps being in formation with the men who were arriving at the Unit's facilities).

The commander (sturmbannführer) another source says hauptsturmführer Ezquerra departed, after conferring in Berlin with Ottlob, for Potsdam with the intention of informing his men. He began by doing so with his non-commissioned officers: Pedro Zabala Urrutia, Ricardo Botet Moro, Enrique Lafuente Barros, Cipriano Sastre Fraile and Lorenzo Ocañas Serrano. They are the non-commissioned officers who make up the Spanish contingent.

Saturday 21 April:

That same morning, the Spanish troops were reviewed, resulting in some 359 men, according to the work of F. Vadillo, "Los Irreductibles", although the figure is logically completely debatable. The troops are informed of the new orders and those who do not wish to participate in the difficult undertaking (by all accounts a defence to the last man in the streets of Berlin) are allowed to return to Spain (if they can do so by their own means) with money and a safe-conduct for the area still occupied by the Germans.

After the harangue made by Commander Ezquerra, highlighting the causes for which many had been fighting since the times of the Blue Division, anti-Bolshevism, the defense of the West against the Soviet hordes, loyalty to the German people in that terrible war. To show what the Spanish soldiers are capable of and how they know how to fight both when the light of victory shines and when the darkness of defeat is on the horizon.

After this emotional harangue, there would be about 34 men who decided not to continue their adventure in the streets of Berlin, preferring the no less complicated adventure of trying to return to Spain.

The men who decided to stay will travel to the very center of Berlin on the U-Bahn (underground railway), still in operation.

After proceeding to embark the troops on the railway, the journey begins, which will have several stops at the stations of Krumme Lanke, Toms Hütte, Helene Heim, Dahlen or Hohenzollern belonging to line 3 of the U-Bahn; following the route on U-Bahn line 1 through stations such as Kurfürsten or Gleisdreieck and ending when they reach the vicinity of Anhalter station. Spaniards will get off the U-Bahn possibly at the station closest to their destination, which corresponds to Gleisdreieck (separating it a few dozen meters from Anhalter station). It will be at this station, after orders received by Ezquerra, where the company under Pedro Zabala will separate from the rest of the men with the order to join the German forces that are trying to regroup in the Alpine redoubt; According to Ezquerra's version, Martín de Arrizubieta was in this group (there are sources that indicate that the separation of Zabala's Company from the rest of the men of the Ezquerra Unit could have taken place on the 18th and they reached their destination at the Rheinigs camp in the Alps on the 29th of April). Upon arriving at the "Alpine Fortress", Zabala's Company found that there was no longer any purpose in continuing the fighting and on April 30 they received the order to go to Italy to try to return to Spain.

After the departure of the 71 men of SS-Obersturmführer Pedro Zabala's Company, the Spanish troops were reduced to two companies. With respect to both groups, one will be under the command of Ezquerra himself and the other under the orders of Ensign Ricardo Botet Moro. This last group will separate from the first, losing contact with the latter during the multiple skirmishes that will take place inside the Berlin capital. This means that finally the men who will make up the Einheit Ezquerra in the defense of Berlin will reach a total of about 130 men (there are sources that would reduce this number to just under a hundred, although it is very difficult to corroborate one version or the other; although it gives us the idea of the small number of Spaniards who took part in the fighting for the capital of the Reich). To these should be added a variable number of men who in one way or another were temporarily under the command of the Ezquerra Unit. In his book, he mentions that about three dozen Belgians belonging to the "Wallonien" joined his fighting force; although, as there is no reference to this fact by any other source (well documented in the case of the "Wallonien"), it is quite doubtful that it happened.

On leaving the station and reaching the surface, our men were able to observe the pitiful state in which the capital was; Blackened and largely ruined buildings, some of them still smoldering, wrecked vehicles, debris, barricades. In a word, it was hell. And the worst was yet to come.

Once formed, and after Botet's departure, Ezquerra's men are housed in an emergency shelter. It was located on the ground floor of a half-ruined building, in a place that in better times was a shoe store. It was in close proximity to the Foreign Ministry, as well as to the area of the ministries.

It is here that Ezquerra narrated "the incorporation into the group of 17 Frenchmen in the uniform of Doriot's militia, as well as 4 Belgians of the SS legion "Wallonie". According to Ezquerra, they were all part of the unit, but distributed among the Spanish soldiers and not as independent units. This fact, as we mentioned, is more than doubtful, since there is no information whatsoever (except Ezquerra's version) that makes us think about the accuracy of this information. Although it is very likely that circumstantially in the heat of the fighting in the German capital, at specific moments, men attached to other units, among which there could well be French or Belgians, were temporarily under the command of the Spanish Unit.

When they arrived in Berlin, because they did not have enough weapons, nor were they suitable for the mission that awaited them, they were provided with a significant amount of weaponry. Among them, the MP40 and MP44 machine guns stand out; as well as the dreaded panzerfaust, pistols, hand grenades, MG42s, etc. Of course, they were also supplied with plenty of ammunition for the various weapons.

Sunday 22nd - Thursday 26th:

During this period, there is practically no data or reports that indicate the "activities" carried out by the men of the Spanish Unit.

The Red Army closes more and more the ring that will strangle Berlin, achieving almost entirely on the 24th, but only at the cost of suffering severe punishment from the defenders of the capital.

On the 23rd they received news that the Russians had entered Potsdam, where approximately fifty Spaniards were still stationed under the command of a sergeant named Cerezo. And although they fight with extreme courage, even reaching close quarters, they mostly perish. It seems that only Cerezo and a few other men manage to survive and break through the Russian lines. But the trail of these men is lost in the whirlwind of the last days of the Reich. These tidings only increase the desire of Ezquerra and his men to confront the Soviets.

Friday 27 April:

Soviet troops advance towards Potsdamer Platz and Alexanderplatz. Ezquerra will fight for the first of these, which is harassed by huge quantities of shells, infantry troops, armored vehicles and artillery of all kinds, among which Stalin's dreaded organs stand out.

After spending a day there, they left the old shoe store after receiving orders from an aviation lieutenant colonel who showed up there to move to their new operations center. It is located in a barracks of the military police (the Reich Security Service, RSD or Reichssicherheitsdienst), quite close to its previous accommodation, much more suitable for accommodating troops. A battalion of SS troops was also housed there.

Finally, they assign him the area where they will have to put their brick in the defensive framework of the city. It will be in the second defensive ring of the existing three. The one located between the suburban circle and the Zitadelle (citadel).

Their first mission is coming up, so the men rest and get their weapons ready. They know that in a short time some of them will have fallen, but even so, their willingness to do their bit in the defense of the capital of the Reich can be seen in the firmness of their gaze and in the imperious desire to confront the enemy as soon as possible.

He arrives at the barracks where the Spanish troops are stationed, a link with the order to present himself to Commander Ezquerra, to indicate the order to present himself to the Chief of the Sector where they are. This was a Lieutenant Colonel of Engineers, whose staff was located in a nearby square which, along with its surrounding buildings, was being subjected to the continuous explosion of Russian shells. This chief, ignoring the intense enemy fire, detailed to Ezquerra the mission that would be entrusted to the Spanish troops, which would consist of repelling the Soviet advance near the area where Moritz Platz is located.

Once the orders are received, Ezquerra relays them to his men, who greet them with shouts and cheers, as they will finally be able to release all the tension they have been accumulating for some time before. They will once again face their old enemies, the Soviets.

Ezquerra gave the order to march to the 1st company, under the command of Sergeant (formerly Ensign Ocañas, although according to "Yo, muerto en Rusia" or "I, Dead in Russia" he would have the rank of SS lieutenant). They advance from the area of the Air Ministry, taking refuge in the walls of the dilapidated buildings that populate the streets, as well as any element that can serve as a shelter against Russian fire. The distance to Moritz Platz was about two kilometers in a southeasterly direction, so they chose to take the fastest route, as the urgency of the situation demanded. This will consist of going from the Wilhelmstrasse to the Stadtmittestrasse and then cutting through the narrowest streets until you reach the Oranienstrasse, at the east end of which was the Square.

Making their way through the multitude of rubble that populates the streets of the centre of Berlin, it takes them about two hours to reach the vicinity of Moritz Platz. Although the rumble of heavy fighting can already be heard in the area, between German forces and combined Soviet armored and infantry troops.

There the Spaniards will be able to see how the boys of the Hitler Youth, who are defending the metro station, fight the copper. They will not cease to amaze Ezquerra and his people as simple children, still of school age, armed mainly with anti-tank weapons, harass the invaders, managing to turn several T-34s into scrap metal and bonfires. Their attitude increases even more the euphoria of the Spaniards, if some kids manage to maintain their positions, what can't they. For many of our men have been fighting for several years.

At the end of the street was the small Moritz Platz, through which the Soviet armor advanced under cover of its infantry.

To the left of the Spanish positions, German troops were sheltered in ruins. Not knowing of the presence of Ezquerra's men, they shot them; which caused them to throw themselves on the ground and return friendly fire. When the two groups finally recognized each other as allies and belonging to the same side, the firing stopped. The reason for the confusion was that the Germans heard voices in a language that was unknown to them and mistook them for Russian troops, and their results in the Unit were the death of three men and two more with severe injuries.

After this event, they continue their advance until they make contact with the enemy, taking by assault the first barricades in which the Russians take cover, while the continuous fire of the tanks resounds over the entire disputed area.

There they are waiting for the new horde of Stalin men and tanks approaching from the south of the Square. Crouching down and after taking defensive positions, they wait for the order of their commander to unleash all the fury of their weapons against the Soviets. They advance cautiously, although they cannot avoid falling into continuous ambushes. Like the one carried out by the Spaniards following Ezquerra's orders. From all sides, shots fall on the Russian infantry who, as they take cover and retreat, leave the field open to the tank hunters, who give a good account of 4 or 5 of the immense IS-2s. It is inevitable that there will be casualties among the men of the Einheit, but they have managed to slow the advance and cause the Russians to retreat. After this clash, the men, by order of Ezquerra, withdrew slightly to reinforce their positions and evacuate the wounded. During the engagement they had sustained, they were reinforced by the addition of Latvian troops to their Unit, as well as possibly some other "wayward" soldier who was temporarily attached to the Unit. But the Russians charge again in less than a quarter of an hour, so all hell fire is unleashed again. Once again, the defenders manage to repel the Soviet armored vehicles (destroying and damaging many of them), which are defenseless when not accompanied by infantry that shoots down the crouching men who stalk with their anti-tank weapons from any pile of rubble, holes in buildings, windows, portals or even sometimes bare-chested.

There are new casualties, this time of at least 6 men, but the spearhead of the Soviet advance is repelled again. Several hours have passed since they arrived at the Square and they have already been able to observe with their own eyes the harshness of the fighting in the face of a huge and inexhaustible Russian army, which attacks again and again without its troops seeming to have an end. Exhaustion is present in all the defenders, so once the area is stabilized, they will be replaced by German SS troops.

This was the first direct contact with the Russian enemy on the streets of Berlin; just a prologue of what would be a coming and going to one area or another, which was in danger. This will lead them to become a real firefighting unit, which will try to stop the fire, wherever it occurs.

They return to the vicinity of the Air Ministry and prepare to regain their strength after the exhausting clashes they had had. But the situation in the Zitadelle sector, with each passing second, is deteriorating. Men are needed in each of the breaches that the Russians are making in the defensive framework, and among other veteran troops, the Spaniards are called upon again. Their new assignment will be to try to recapture the bridge next to Belle Alliance Platz over the Landwehr canal, which was being assaulted by the Russians. Its loss will mean the way free of natural obstacles from the south of the Soviet troops, and leaving in their path the main official buildings of Berlin, headed by the New Chancellery in whose bunker, Hitler directs, or at least tries to, the defense of the capital.

They advance along Leipziger Strasse in the direction of Leipziger Platz, and from there they will regain Wilhelmstrasse, which is currently under heavy artillery fire. Sometimes it becomes impossible to go down the street, so the men have to advance through the buildings, by making holes in the walls that separate them from each other, as well as taking advantage of the basements of the same to progress towards their goal. Due to the increasing difficulties of advancing even through the buildings, they decide to head towards Anhalter Station. Thousands of people take refuge in it from the swell that floods the city, who see how these soldiers, who carried a red-yellow-red flag in their arms, go bravely to meet the enemy. Although all seems lost, the willingness and good spirit of the Spaniards allows a sigh of relief, albeit quite short-lived, to many of the refugees.

Ezquerra plans to reach the vicinity of Belle Alliance Platz, via the metro tunnels that start from Anhalter station. These are in complete darkness in most of their sections, so they will advance with the light of the few lanterns carried by the officers and in rows of two, so as not to lose contact with each other.

They come back to the surface via the Möckernbrucke U-Bahn, so they will have to advance more than a kilometer in an easterly direction to reach their goal.

The Belle Alliance Platz is a crossroads bordering the Landwehr Canal to the south, which is crossed by a bridge, over which the Soviet outposts are already peeking out again. The whole area is being subjected to a continuous bombardment, where the fire of cannons, large caliber mortars and the katiuskas demolish everything in their path. But the defenders, well sheltered, resist the strong push of the Russians. From the various streets that lead to the square, more and more troops come; from the north the Germans and from the south the Soviets. The din of combat can be felt from where the Spaniards are cautiously but accelerating their march, approaching the square. They advance covered by the walls of the buildings on the street that runs parallel to the canal, taking advantage of the multitude of debris that is in it, as defenses against the enemy fire that rages from the other bank. In a few minutes they manage to reach their destination, where the fire is now more intense, since only a few hundred meters further south are the Soviets. Our men join the defense of the northern end of the bridge, still in German hands. There they have the chance to test the mettle of the Hitler Youth boys, since they were in charge of defending many of Berlin's bridges.

Infantry advance across the bridge in conjunction with the tanks, firing incessantly. They are answered by a fire, not as forceful as the Soviet one, but very accurate, since it is concentrated in the area of the bridge. At least half a dozen tanks manage to point their guns towards Wilhelmstrasse.

The Spaniards on the left side of the beginning of the bridge, protected by the remains of buildings, go on the attack. At the height of the battle, by chance, they find another Spaniard in a German regiment, which will eventually be added to the Einheit. This is Ismael Múgica, who will become one of Ezquerra's trusted men, both for his extensive knowledge of the fighting in the streets, and for the German language, according to Ezquerra himself in his story.

Three of the advancing tanks were aiming for their positions, still firing. A trio of men, including Sastre, Vázquez and Múgica, advanced against the walls of the buildings. After that, another group of men advanced, among them was Ezquerra. In this exchange of fire and as he approached the tanks with his panzerfaust, Vázquez was wounded. His comrades managed to rescue him, risking their lives to save their comrade under the continuous pounding of Russian automatic weapons.

The final result was that, thanks to the use of panzerfausts, one of the shells hit the first armored vehicle, causing an explosion that caused the destruction of the tank and its occupants. The same path is followed by 3 more Russian tanks, which will also be knocked out thanks to the powerful effect of the panzerfaust. The remainder, finding themselves without infantry support, opted for a strategic retreat.

Soon the Russians are back at it, and with renewed troops they manage to get over the bridge with their armored outposts. Some of the first houses on the north bank were occupied by the Russians in the face of their powerful push, allowing them to take positions and become strong in them.

Ezquerra's men, along with other groups of German soldiers, will take on the difficult task of dislodging them. In this confrontation, Ezquerra's ankle is damaged, when he falls through a hole into a basement, which due to the recent explosion of a grenade has burning embers. After being taken out of there with the help of his comrades, he will be evacuated to be properly cared for, as far as circumstances allow, in the sanitary facilities located in the Excelsior Hotel. In Ezquerrra's absence, it will be Lieutenant Múgica who will take over the command of the Spanish Unit.

Meanwhile, the rest of the men of the Unit will maintain their positions, since hand-to-hand combat has been going on in some areas for a long time now. But hundreds and hundreds of Russians continue their advance despite the multitude of casualties they suffer, as these are supplied by more and more reinforcements. But the German resistance is fanatical and allows them to stop this new blow, after having lost a good number of meters in each Russian counterattack. Because of this coming and going from the front line, a small number of German troops are behind the enemy lines, among whom are Spaniards and some boys from the Hitler Youth. Now they will have to make use of their weapons so as not to fall victim to the increasingly intense enemy fire or be captured by the increasingly abundant Russian troops. After intense hand-to-hand fighting, and with good fortune, they will manage to return to German-dominated territory.

Finally, after coming out of that mousetrap, according to Ezquerra, they count the casualties, both dead and missing, among which are the brave ones, Sergeant Carlos Ramos Valdevalles, Eugenio Álvarez Valdecasas, César García Pesquera, Luis Ángel Casado Aspe and Miguel Ramírez Jarama.

After that, the survivors, exhausted from a whole day of fighting, as well as the continuous tension of being continuously subjected to the uninterrupted fire of the Soviets, who will turn the Berlin sky into gloomy and full of smoke, which is sometimes almost unbreathable, make their way back to their barracks.

Once again, the Spanish troops will have their place of lodging changed. From now on, they will reside in the premises of the Air Ministry. This is a large Prussian-style building that occupies the corner of Leipzig and Wilhelm streets, and is close to Leipziger Platz, once an important social life, today turned into land devastated by continuous bombardments, with many semi-collapsed buildings and rubble everywhere. To prevent the civilian population from being exposed to the rigors of war, they are being housed in multiple shelters, among which the ministry's own shelter stands out for its large size, which can accommodate thousands and thousands of people.

Saturday 28 April:

The struggles are more constant and with fewer intervals with each passing day. Exhaustion weighs on the combatants, although the defenders have the upper hand, since for them there are no replacements, as is the case with the troops of the Red Army. Although the fighting has been intense in the previous days, from this morning the battle will reach its peak and will remain at this level until the end.
The Spanish troops, scattered after so many vicissitudes, are in the Anhalterplatz (where they fight side by side with other men, among whom are the decimated troops of the Müncheberg division and the Nordland), in the area of the Alexanderplatz, the stations of Anhalter and Potsdam, the Herman Göring strasse. In all these places they resist with their automatic weapons and their panzerfausts.
There is no order, they simply fight and resist at one point, until they are finally dislodged from it due to the incessant fire of cannons and mortars that literally crush the positions of the defenders. And again, at the next corner, the same operation, waiting for the enemy armor on some ruined wall without firing their weapons until the last second. Although with less and less room to go back.
Whenever possible, the city's defenders used the scarce German armor to move from one place to another. In this regard, we have this impression left to us by a Spanish SS-Sturmann named Horacio E.:
"Whenever we could, we climbed on the tanks so we didn't have to walk, we were very crowded together and held on to each other so we didn't fall over the potholes. I remember a boy we called "el Asturiano" who had a large shield of Spain sewn on his arm and who, in one of those potholes, slipped on the right side of the tank with the bad luck of getting caught in the chains, gave terrible screams while his leg detached from his body at the level of the groin. It was in a few seconds but they seemed eternal to me, we couldn't do anything for him, he bled to death a short time later. "
The Russians advance inexorably, arriving with their armored vehicles accompanied by infantry troops along Wilhelmstrasse, to the vicinity of the Air Ministry itself.
In this area, defenders accumulate along with troops retreating from different points of the front. A front that is only a few meters in front of them and behind them. At the end of the day, numerous bomb craters render the Friedrichstrasse roads impassable.
At dawn, his liaison sergeant and interpreter from the Einheit informs Ezquerra of the news. The men were relieved by SS troops from the square where the day before they had faced the Soviet advances. After that, they were again ordered to concentrate in the basements of the Air Ministry.
Once Ezquerra rejoined his men and after a short rest, they were entrusted with a Latvian battalion (under the command of Commander Willi, although according to the book "David against Goliath: Latvian volunteers in the Waffen SS (1941-1945)" by Carlos Caballero it would correspond to the name of Wallis), the mission of stopping the Soviet outposts wherever they appeared.
Their position was close to the elegant Hotel Excelsior, between the Ministry of the Army and the Chancellery, near Potsdamer Platz and the rest of the ministries. The hotel was connected by subway to the Potsdamer station, which in this situation favored the transfer from one part to another, avoiding the continuous enemy fire that the streets of Berlin endured. The appearance of Potsdamer Platz was unsettling, covered with wrecked vehicles, mutilated bodies and wounded people struggling to find shelter at the nearby station.
The head of the sector, in telephone contact with Commander Willi, ordered that Ezquerra's men should move to the area of the Kaiserhof Hotel. Since the distance to that point was quite short (a few hundred meters), despite the intense fire that fell on the Zitadelle, it was not a difficult task. Once they arrived in the area, the men took up positions throughout the Hotel area, as well as within the hotel.
Ezquerra distributed men at the strategic points of the project, awaiting the prompt arrival of the Russian advance guards arriving from the southeast. The atmosphere in the hotel was completely dreamlike. Here people continued to live with the same luxury and artificiality as in the now distant time of peace. Not surprisingly, it was still attended by large gyrfalcons, diplomats, journalists and civilians of high social status, as

well as high-ranking military officials. Of course, there was an abundance of smartly dressed women, artists, cabaret girls, luxury prostitutes, as well as food items that were no longer or were never in the pantries of the Berlin population, among which the finest French wines and champagne stood out.

Outside these walls, the Russians were approaching the area, this time advancing from Kronen Street. They are reconnaissance groups, and behind them come tanks, mainly T34s and the powerful IS2. The Spanish, French and Belgian soldiers who are in that area, go back to the Russian incursion area, stationing themselves in the nearby houses with their anti-tank weapons, MG42s, assault rifles, and finally with all their weapons available. From positions sometimes impossible for the Soviets to locate, due to the multitude of debris that populates the streets, they were stopped temporary.

After finishing off the Russian infantrymen with a heavy fire, some man has the courage and an absolute contempt for life, enough to get as close as possible with his panzerfaust to each tank in order to deal a final blow to their most vital parts. They were already well taught at the time that these areas were located in the turret, at its base and in the part close to the driver of the car. With the T-34 it was difficult, but the work multiplied when it came to facing that 46-ton armored monster that was the IS2. Despite this, after a battle that lasted at least 2 hours, the result was 5 tanks knocked out, as well as dozens of men killed and wounded on both sides. One of the Spanish men of the Einheit, nicknamed the "chato", left the only 3 tanks turned into scrap metal, Múgica finished with another and the fifth by Sergeant Ferrer.

After this battle, the Russians retreated again, but not without having advanced a few meters from their original starting position, narrowing more and more the pincer that "suffocated" Berlin. Once the positions were left to fresh troops, Ezquerra's men made a reconnaissance to Hans Vogtei Platz.

In this advance there is no sign of any movement of the enemy, so strategic positions are taken with a view to probable new Soviet attacks. Hours later, when the Soviet attack was quelled, the small Spanish unit was again relieved by a German refreshment battalion.

So, commanded by Ezquerra, they marched to the Air Ministry, where Ezquerra received new orders, which consisted of participating in the defense of the entire area of the ministries, located between Herman Göring and Friedrich streets up to Unter den Linden. They immediately depart for their new place of deployment together with Willi's Latvian soldiers, to repel a raid perpetrated by two Soviet infantry battalions accompanied by several tanks that are dangerously close to Potsdamer Platz. Ezquerra's men and the Latvians begin to advance in the direction of the square, but this path will be slowed down by the continuous explosions of bombs of all types and calibers. Overcoming this danger (not without suffering at least 5 casualties), they managed to gain access to the vicinity of the square, where they began to take up positions mainly in semi-ruined buildings. From there the soldiers aim their panzerfaust and small arms at the armored and infantry respectively, which begin to fill the square. The tactics used in these situations are quite similar to those used on other occasions, they wait hidden until the target is close enough to be able to welcome them according to the circumstances. No one moves, they keep their fingers on the triggers and triggers of their panzerfaust, until the first armor is in firing position.

After quelling this new attack, the men, visibly fatigued after a long day of continuous tensions, return to their base in the Air Ministry. The destruction that was evident in the city was absolute. Collapsed houses, ruins in all the streets and deaths, many dead both civilians and soldiers who were immersed in a spiral of blood and death that seemed to have no end. In this regard, there is the impression on this matter of Julio Botet's liaison, SS-Schütze Julio L.:

"I felt hatred and rage, pity for myself and pleasure when I killed, but most of all I felt an atrocious panic of losing any limb of my body, all of Berlin was a dumping ground for human limbs torn apart by bombs and shrapnel. I remember that a German from another unit, I think it was from the Luftwaffe and I were stationed very close to the entrance of the subway, when we saw a woman on the other side of the street with a child in her arms who was about to cross, the German was shouting at her not to move because we were in a beaten area, Either she didn't understand us or she didn't listen to us, the point is that she ran towards us, she wouldn't take more than three steps when a grenade exploded in front of her, the blast wave threw her towards us as if she were a rag doll, she sat up stunned almost naked and bleeding all over, the child was decapitated and what was left of the body was a mass of flesh, The poor woman, between moans and cries, began the macabre task of looking for the child's head, we were indifferent, we didn't care about everything."

Sunday 29 April:

The new orders received by Ezquerra consisted of taking up positions in the area where the Reichsbank was located. The unit moves slowly along the sides of the streets, sheltering behind the remains of the smoldering buildings. Finally, they reach the vicinity of the Reichsbank, where they observe how a company of Russian infantry troops are trying to encircle it. Inside the bank, in a hodgepodge of defending troops, many boys from the Hitler Youth stand out. These, on many occasions, present a firmness that many men have lost after so many years of combat.

The men of the Einheit, who are more than firm, despite having only had a few hours of rest on them in the last three days, attack the Russians from the flank, managing to break their line of advance and causing them to retreat with many casualties.

All the action unfolds in a short time, it's close to dawn, and they deserve a break. But it is not possible, because they are immediately reclaimed to the area where Potsdam Platz is located, which is suffering a severe attack by combined infantry and armored forces. They come under cover of the buildings in the streets that access the square and are located in the defensive positions maintained by the German troops. They remain there for several hours, until finally, once the new day dawns, they are summoned to another sector in extreme danger of falling under the Russian roller. Their new destination will be a few hundred meters to the east, in the area of the Kaiserhof hotel, according to Ezquerra.

When they arrive at the hotel, the tasks of "cleaning" begin, filling new positions, etc. Due to the gloom that exists in these early hours of the morning, they have to use flashlights to locate enemies.

During the early hours of the morning in extreme temperature conditions, a small group of Spaniards, led by Ezquerra, rest for a few minutes in the ruins of the old majestic Europa cinema. This cinema has a corridor that leads to Anhalterplatz, which must be recognized. Ezquerra orders Lieutenant Lorenzo Ocañas to have one of his men carry out this task of discovery. The chosen one will be Macario Vallejo, who heads towards the corridor in darkness. Minutes that seem like hours pass, and shouts in Russian and the rattle of machine guns can be heard in the distance. Fearing the worst, Ocañas rushes down the hallway following Vallejo's footsteps. When he reaches the outside, he also falls into the ambush of the Russians, who manage to capture him. The results for the unit are 4 dead and one missing (Ocañas). After his capture, Ocañas was taken to the basement of the Excelsior Hotel, held by the Russians, who use it as their command post. After intense interrogations, Ocañas managed to save his life, only to remain 10 years in captivity in miserable conditions in prison camps in the Soviet Union, until he was finally repatriated on the ship Semiramis in 1954.

The men, exhausted after long hours of practically uninterrupted combat, return to their "base" of the Air Ministry, where they will rest anywhere they can find.

Throughout this day, contacts are maintained with the Russians, where it is agreed to make contact with them to parley. Unsurprisingly, due to the intransigence of both sides, they do not reach any agreement. For the Russians want a surrender in all order, to which the exhausted German troops flatly refuse. Here, as Ezquerra tells us in his book, he also participated as an exceptional guest himself. He claims to have been one of the members of the group of German parliamentarians sent to negotiate with the Russians. Also speaking in favor of this fact is what Lieutenant Ocañas said in his book about his encounter with Ezquerra, when the lieutenant was already a captive, as well as Ezquerra's attempt to take him to the German lines, although without success due to the refusal of the Soviets. Whether this meeting is true or not (although there are, as we mentioned, data that seem to give it plausibility), what is known is that any attempt at negotiation in these days resulted in the same as the one discussed here.

Monday 30 April:

The Einheit resists in the vicinity of Potsdam Square, taking refuge in any hole, pile of rubble, abandoned vehicles or anything that can be used for it. With the slogan of not taking "one step backwards", they resist attacks, but when it no longer makes sense to remain and only at that moment does Ezquerra authorize the retreat through metro tunnels following the remnants that still resist of the Müncheberg division, which shortly before had used them to flee the area.

Some of the Spaniards, in their retreat with the Soviet troops on their backs, retreated along Friedrichstrasse, taking up positions in the vicinity of the Chancellery, in whose bunker, Adolf Hitler committed suicide that same day.

Tuesday 1 May:

Ezquerra and the few who follow him, as well as other scattered groups of Spanish soldiers, begin the defense of the ministerial quarter, in continuous struggle for every property in the limited Berlin territory that still remains in the hands of the Germans.
The Russians approach from Wilhelmstrasse and Friedrichstrasse.
The remnants of the unit go on to defend the area of the Ministry of the Interior, together with the remains of many other units such as the Nordland or the Müncheberg. The building is defended, as usual, meter by meter. Every room is a death trap for the Russians, which only serves to delay the inevitable by a few more hours.
The remnants of the Einheit are gathered at the Air Ministry, after a day of continuous fighting and retreats. There, Captain Willi conveyed to Ezquerra an order of great importance that he had received shortly before from the Führerbunker itself. These consist of forming, with their men and with the remnants of Latvian troops who are still in a position to fight, a group that will try to break the encirclement to which they are subjected by the Russians.
Discreetly, they leave the positions they occupy and head towards the Air Ministry, the meeting point for these troops. There, at the Air Ministry, Ezquerra confirms to his men where they will have to advance and where they will be destined, the Stettiner Bahnhof, which is located in a northerly direction, beyond the Spree.
They leave the Air Ministry through the garage and head outwards towards Wilhelm Street. There, taking cover among the rubble and the walls of the adjoining buildings, they advance towards the nearby metro station, which is a short distance from the ministry. From this station, protected by the underground tunnels, they manage to reach the next station of Wilhelmplatz. There, Ezquerra's men regroup, arriving little by little intermingled with their Latvian comrades.
Finally, an SS colonel manages to order the different groups of soldiers arriving at the station and informs them of the next meeting point; which will be the Friedrichstrasse station next to the Spree. After a good walk in which they negotiate various obstacles in the tunnels, as well as some corpses of unfortunates who ended their days there, they finally arrive at the Friedrichstrasse station.
The north bank of the Weidendamm Bridge was at that time the northern front line of Berlin and had to be crossed in order to reach the destination that our men have fixed; the Stettiner Bahnhof. The four Spaniards who miraculously were still fighting in the Spanish Unity and not without a good dose of luck, managed to cross the bridge to pass immediately to the shelter offered by the first houses that are to the left of it. Men from various units join them on a strictly temporary basis, in order to try to achieve their common goal: the very close and at the same time so distant Stettiner Bahnhof. Finally, from these houses, in just a few meters they manage to reach their goal. The last order that the Einheit received has been carried out, at the cost of losing all its men except for its chief and Pinar.
In spite of the short distance that separated them from her, they reached the bunker of the Stettiner Bahnhof, where there were still some German fighting troops, under the command of which they placed themselves. It will be there that they are finally captured by the Russians. During this day, most of the Unit's men had fallen in the fighting, but it was all over for the few survivors.
Specifically, Ezquerra, after spending several days in captivity, managed to escape from the poorly guarded groups of prisoners. After multiple vicissitudes and posing as one of the thousands of forced laborers that the Germans had had in their territory, he reached Spain through the Pyrenees.
Among the lucky few who were able to return to their homeland, the only thing left was to try to remain anonymous, or run the risk, as happened to some men, of being subjected to a War Council for "abandonment of destiny", as a result of disobeying the regulations issued by the Spanish government in this regard. Although this man was acquitted a couple of years later.

▲ Ricardo Botet Moro was one of the most active Spaniards in the German armed forces, having served in the Blue Division, the Blue Legion, the SD, the 28th SS-Freiwilligen-Panzergrenadier-Division 'Wallonien' and the Ezquerra Unit. Courtesy of Almena and Augusto Ferrer-Dalmau.

▲ One of the few pictures of Spaniards in SS uniform. This is SS-Oscha Camargo (left in the photo) in the spring of 1945 near Rodengo-Saiano, in the Brescia area, during manoeuvres with his unit: the I./WGRsSS81, part of the 29th Waffen Grenadier Division der SS. Courtesy of Erik Norling.

▼ Officers of the SS Wallonien Division pose for the photographer at the officers' school in Kienschlag (Botet also attended this school), among them is Spaniard Lorenzo Oca.as (6) who participated with the Ezquerra Unit in the Battle of Berlin, where he was captured. The names of some SS members accompanying Oca.as in the photo are known, such as Serlet (1), Suain (2), Foulon (3), De Goy (4) and Hancisse (5). Courtesy of Almena and Augusto Ferrer-Dalmau.

▲ The only publicly known photograph of Miguel Ezquerra, taken in 1982 in an interview for the magazine Interviú. Image kindly provided by Interviú magazine through its editor-in-chief Aitor Marín for reproduction in this book.

REPATRIATION

The process of returning to Spain was very complicated. The circumstances of the occupation, both by the Soviet Union and by the Western allies of the former Reich, in addition to the destruction of a large part of its infrastructure, did not allow for a smooth movement through its lands.

The first part of the return of the men who survived from the Ezquerra Unit, was to flee the Soviet occupation zone to the side of the Western Allies. Membership in the SS would prove to be an element against the Spaniards in the western sector, but it could mean immediate death in the eastern sector. Shortly before the capitulation, several Spaniards (among whom, according to Ezquerra, there were about thirty members of his Unit) managed to leave Berlin and later Germany, thanks to the help of the Spanish Consulate in Berlin. Other groups of Spaniards (possibly those who remained in the Alpine area) after being exempted from their oath of allegiance to Hitler, received passports to neutral Switzerland, where they would be imprisoned in the camps of Oerlikon-Zurich and Laplaine-Geneva. These, after the corresponding authorizations, obtained through the mediation of the Government of Spain a train that would leave from Bern and arrive at the French station of Chambery on June 17. While at this station, the train was assaulted by forces of the former maquis and had to return to Switzerland; They were again interned in the camps of Laplaine-Geneva and Bühler-Apenzell. They would have to wait until December 3 when they managed to return to Spain aboard the ship "Plus Ultra".

Another group of Spaniards was the one who, after being captured by the Western Allies, had to go through some concentration camps until they were later liberated. These are the cases of some of the men who had served under the orders of Lieutenant Ortiz (who belonged to the 102nd) and had remained in the mountains of northern Italy without passing through Stockerau, such as Antonio Pardo (who was taken prisoner in Udine and held until October 1948) or Federico Martínez (captured in Gorizia and held in Rimini until July 1949 when he escaped and returned to Spain clandestinely by Puigcerdá). Other men who served in the Wehrmacht managed to reach Rome (with the connivance of the Italian population) and from there managed to be repatriated to Spain.

But many Spaniards had been held captive by the Soviets and conditions would not be the same. In the "gulags" they had to survive for hard years that seemed to have no end, subjected to all kinds of humiliations and deprivations.

After Stalin's death in March 1953, the living conditions of the captives improved and rumors of possible repatriation began to circulate. A year later, the captives were concentrated in the port of Odessa, of whom 18 decided to stay on their own accord in the U.S.S.R., as well as 65 deserters who, for fear of reprisals, would not return to their homeland either. On Friday, April 2, 1954, the Spanish prisoners of war who, after being held captive for 10 or 12 years in the Soviet Gulags with infinite hardships, had managed to survive, returned to Spain after contacts between the Soviet and Spanish governments. This long-awaited return took place on the Liberian-flagged Greek ship "Semiramis", chartered by Spain at the expense of the Red Cross, which departing from the port of Odessa, will disembark 286 people in the port of Barcelona. These would be distributed according to their origin, as follows in the most truthful way:

A contingent of 248 prisoners of war consisted of:

- 219 men who had belonged to the Spanish Division of
  Volunteers (DEV).
- 7 to the Spanish Legion of Volunteers (LEV).
- 21 to Waffen SS.
- 1 to the "Blue" Squadron.

The remaining contingent of 38 people was divided as follows:

- 4 "Children of War".
- 34 boarding schools. These, in turn, were distributed:

- 19 sailors, most of them crew members of the motor ship "Cabo San Agustín", a ship that transported shipments of gold from the Bank of Spain to Odessa. There were also sailors from the Republican Fleet who, at the end of the Spanish Civil War, were in Soviet territory.
- 12 men who had been students at the Kirovavad Aviation School and who, after the end of the Spanish Civil War, did not renounce their Spanish citizenship, being declared dissidents and interned in camps.
- 3 workers imprisoned in Germany at the end of World War II.

(data obtained from the article published in number 46 of the excellent "Revista Española de Historia Militar" with the title "Semiramis, 1954: The return of the captives of the Blue Division").

It will be at 5:35 a.m. that day when the ship docks in the port, disembarking some thin and emaciated men after such a long captivity, thus concluding their "adventure" in their fight against the Soviets. Of the total number of returnees, about twenty were men who had been integrated into the Waffen SS.
There they were greeted by a large crowd of people, including family members and other close friends. On behalf of the Head of State, the Minister Secretary General of the Movement, Raimundo Fernández Cuesta, and the Minister of the Army, Lieutenant General Muñoz Grandes (first head of the Blue Division), accompanied by Agustín Aznar, National Delegate for Health, came on board to welcome the Movement. A thanksgiving ceremony is held in the Basilica of La Merced, with the Archbishop-Bishop of Barcelona, Modrego, present. Although the "Semiramis" did not bring all the prisoners who remained in the U.S.S.R., since until 1955 it is known that a number of Spaniards were still alive that is difficult to determine. In fact, one of the men who fought in the Ezquerra Unit in the Battle of Berlin, Juan Pinar, who was released in December 1955. Despite the bad relations between the Soviet and Spanish governments, thanks to the mediation of the Red Cross, some 2500 Spaniards were repatriated in seven "trips" between September 1956 and May 1959 (in the months of September, October, November and December 1956; January and May 1957; May 1959) which were mostly made by the ship "Crimea" and bound for the port of Castellón. But these other returnees, due to Spain's situation in the world at that time, have gone almost unnoticed over the years until today, without having had their "moment" of glory in the newspapers or news of the time. Among all these returnees, there were few men belonging to the DEV, one belonging to the Waffen SS having been captured in Yugoslavia, possibly a member of the 102nd Company.

▲ A guard of honour accompanies the coffin of a fallen divisionary being transported by a carriage through Russian territory (LET).

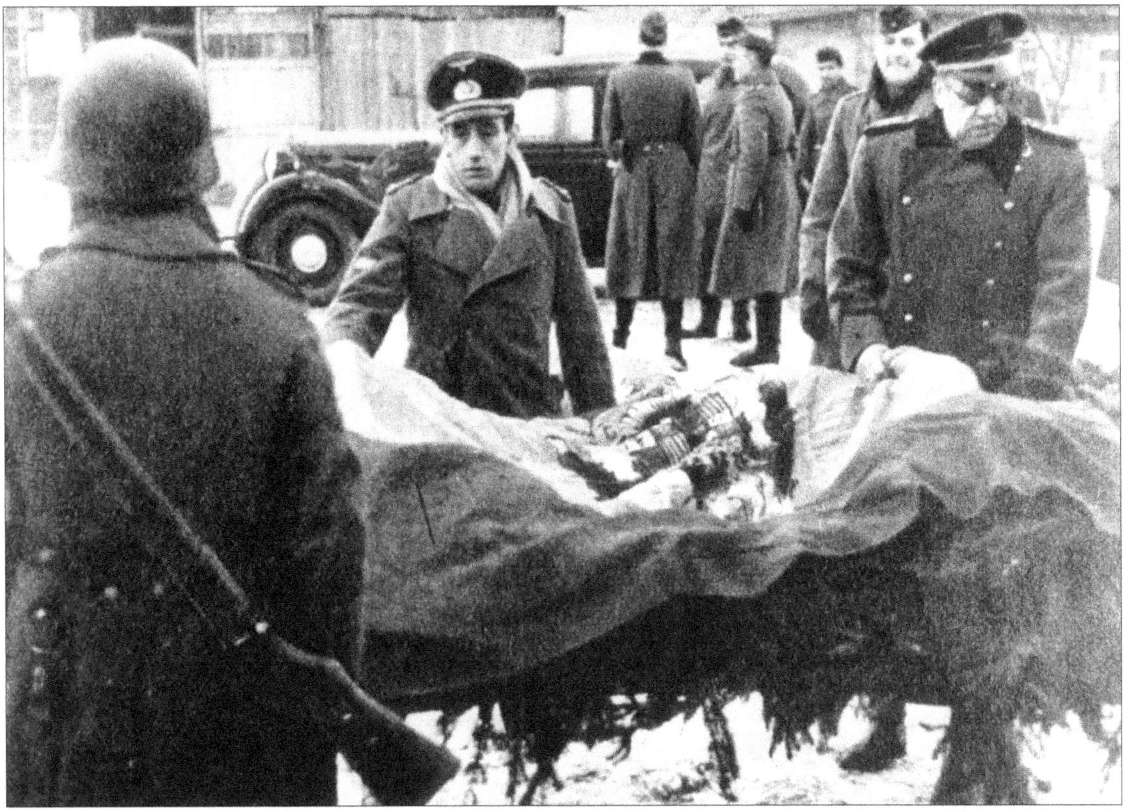

▲ General Moscardó visited the DEV under the command of Muñoz Grandes between November and December 1941. There he attended the burial of one of the Spanish fallen (LET).

▼ A sad farewell to a comrade on Russian soil (LET).

▲ German and Spanish flags cover the coffins where the bodies of divisionaries who fell in the fight against the Soviets rest (LET).

▼ General Esteban Infantes at the funeral of a divisionary (LET).

▲ 'I had a comrade...' (LET).

▼ '... of all, the best' (LET).

▲ Commotion at the Königsberg hospital cemetery (LET).

▼ Not all divisionaries were able to receive a proper burial as in the photo, due to the heavy pressure exerted by the Soviets on the Hispanic-German defence lines (LET).

▲ Soviet women attend the burial of DEV soldiers. The Spaniards' good treatment of the Soviet civilian population allowed the development of certain emotional bonds between them (LET).

▼ The cemetery in Riga, where men of various nationalities are buried. who served in the German Armed Forces (LET).

▲ The return of returnees on the Semíramis was experienced 'in situ' by thousands of people in Barcelona (LET).

▲ The deck and bridge of the Semíramis with eager Spaniards, eager to return home after years of captivity (LET).
▼ Emotion can be read on the faces of the Spanish returnees on board the Semíramis (LET).

▲ Muñoz Grandes at the reception of returnees on the Semíramis at the Ministry of the Army (LET).

▼ Muñoz Grandes giving a welcome speech to returnees on Semíramis (LET).

▲ Another picture of the reception at the Army Ministry for returnees on the Semíramis in 1954 (LET).

▲ Army officers pose in front of a Junkers Ju 52 after completing the Air Artillery Observer Course (LET).

▼ Former DEV members parade in Palma de Mallorca in the 1970s (LET).

▲ Burial with full honours of Captain General Muñoz Grandes, who died on 11 July 1970 (LET).
▼ Photograph of the arrival in Barcelona of Blue Division prisoners on the Semíramis (BVD).

▲ Banner presiding over the DEV field hospital, called the 250th Infantry Division of the Wehrmacht (LET).

UNIFORMS

The trip to Germany

When the Blue Division was organized in Spain, most of the volunteers were from two different backgrounds, each with a different type of uniform. The volunteers from the militias of the Falange and on the other hand the members of the Spanish Army.
The Falangist volunteers wore a uniform with jacket and trousers in "beige" (only those who were chiefs, officers and non-commissioned officers wore the military green color), while the members of the army wore the regulation green (khaki) uniform.
All members of the Blue Division wore a red beret.
Most of the volunteers of the Falange and some of the members of the Army wore a blue shirt (typical of the Falange).
With these uniforms, the Spaniards would arrive at the Grafenwöhr camp, where they would receive their new German uniforms.

Blue Division and Blue Legion

The uniforms received at Grafenwöhr were the same as those worn by members of the Wehrmacht. Each Spaniard received a foldable cap, helmet, jacket, trousers, cape and boots. Because of their membership in the Wehrmacht, the men of the Blue Division carried the Wehrmacht eagle (Hoitszeichen) in their right jacket pocket. The only difference with the uniforms of his German comrades was the existence of a shield on the right arm with the colors red-yellow-red and the word SPAIN on it (this shield was also worn on the capes and on the right side of the helmet).
Unofficially, many of the Spanish soldiers continued to wear the blue shirt under their jackets, just as many soldiers who in Spain had belonged to the Spanish Legion wore light green shirts.
When winter came, the Spanish troops were given reversible anoraks (white on one side and camouflaged fabric on the other), as well as white blouses and trousers (to be worn over the green uniform of the Wehrmacht). During this period, it was common for helmets to be painted white for better masking on the cold Russian front. On these blouses and anoraks, on many occasions the shields were sewn with the colors of the Spanish flag despite not being regulated.
When the Blue Division was repatriated, the soldiers had to surrender all uniforms to the German army and revert to the uniforms with which they left Spain for Germany.
When the Blue Division left, the Blue Legion was made up of members of the Division, so the uniforms do not differ from those used by both units.

Wehrmacht and Waffen SS

Once the Blue Legion left for Spain, the Spaniards who continued to fight did so mainly integrated into Wehrmacht and Waffen SS units, wearing the same uniforms worn by their German comrades.
As a curiosity, we relate below the uniforms used by the last Spanish unit in combat: the Ezquerra Unit (Einheit Ezquerra).
The uniforms worn by the men of the Ezquerra unit, because of the situation in Germany at that time, were very heterogeneous. Quartermaster was practically non-existent, so in the ranks of the Einheit, "green" SS uniforms would be interspersed with camouflaged ones of various models or even some of the Wehrmacht. In any case, the Spaniards were supplied in Potsdam with M 44 speckled camouflage uniforms, which consisted of a four-pocket jacket very similar to the Feldbluse M 43 and tube-shaped trousers, both with rayon fabric printed in five colours (various shades of green and brown).
Some of the men still had their blue shirts, which had already been used in common clothes, under the uniforms of German origin used by the men who made up the Blue Division. This shirt was the JONS FE gar-

ment and was used continuously despite breaking the increasingly less strict rules (at the end of the conflict) regarding military clothing. There are also texts that speak of the use of some elements of the uniform of the Spanish army, such as the regulation belt of the Spanish Legion. As for footwear, except for a few who kept their high boots, the most common thing at that point in the conflict were short boots with gaiters.

The belts used in principle were the regulation belts in the SS, although none of them can be ruled out of the Wehrmacht. There are also accounts of former legionaries of the Tercio who still wore their belts with the arquebus and crossbow, as well as their leather wristbands.

The headwear used were the model 35/40 and 42 helmet with and without decals or the peaked cap introduced in 1943 for its greater comfort.

But the truth is that, since there are no known photographs of our men in the Battle of Berlin, all that is known is from accounts made by the survivors and witnesses who existed. Although in general and like other formations of foreigners who fought integrated into the German armed forces, they would be uniformed like the rest of the German fighters, and more specifically like those belonging to the Waffen SS who fought in Berlin as the men of the 33rd SS Division Waffen-Grenadier der SS (Französische nº 1) Charlemagne.

The peculiarities that our men would wear was the shield on the left sleeve (as was the regulation in the Waffen SS) with the national colors and the word "Spain" at the top. Possibly not all men wore it due to the different origins of the troops of the Ezquerra Unit (most of those who had passed through the Division or the Blue Legion did), as well as that in many cases it was attached to the uniform by simple unsewn pins. Although sometimes the shield was placed on the right sleeve, in contravention of the established ordinance. Within this shield, there were several varieties, on which a yoke could be embroidered with arrows, an Iron Cross or swastikas.

On the location of the shield was to be found the regulation eagle of the Waffen SS, in the bosom of which the Spanish Unit was integrated.

Other additions that could be seen in the uniforms would be the bands on the right arm indicating that they have destroyed an armored vehicle in combat; as well as Spanish or German decorations (these in the case of former members of the Blue Division or the Blue Legion) that each one possessed or emblems of the Falange or the SEU.

As another element to consider in the varied appearance that our soldiers could have at that time, it is necessary to keep in mind regarding the volunteers from the Legion who used to wear belts of the Tercio, leather wristbands and a rosary of decorations distributed throughout the warrior. Obviously, we can't generalize about this.

AWARDS

It is not really known how many medals the men of the Unit may have worn on their uniforms but bearing in mind that many of them had already participated in numerous combats either in units under Spanish or German command during the Second World War; as well as possible decorations obtained in Spain during his time in the army.

Let us remember as information of interest, the number of medals obtained by the men members of the Blue Division, of which some took their steps in the Ezquerra Unit, was a Knight's Cross with Oak Leaves, a Knight's Cross, two Gold Crosses, 2497 Iron Crosses (of which 138 were First Class), 2216 Crosses of Military Merit with Swords (of which 16 were First Class).

In addition, it appears that the men who participated in the defense of Berlin mostly received the Iron Cross Second Class for participating in that combat.

▲ DA volunteer Jaime Vallespinosa Solanellas (NEG).

EQUIVALENCE OF WAFFEN SS AND WEHRMACHT RANKS WITH THOSE OF THE SPANISH ARMY

RANK[1]		EQUIVALENCE
WAFFEN SS	**WEHRMACHT**	
TROOP		
SS grenadiers	Schütze	Soldier
SS-Obergrenadier	Oberschütze	Private 1st class
SS-Sturmann (SS-Strm)		Corporal
SS-Rottenführer (SS-Rttf)	Gefreiter	Corporal
SUBOFFICER		
SS-Unterscharführer (SS-Uscha)	Obergefreiter	Sergeant
SS-Scharführer (SS-Scha)	Untoffizier	1st Sergeant
SS-Oberscharführer (SS-Oscha)	Unterfeldwebel	Brigade
	Feldwebel	Company Sergeant
SS-Hauptscharführer (SS-Hascha)	Oberfeldwebel	Second Lieutenant
	Hauptfeldwebel	Regimental Sergeant Major
SS-Sturmscharfhürer (SS-Stscha)	Stabfeldwebel	Senior NCO
OFFICERS		
SS-Untersturmführer (SS-Ustuf)	Leutnant	Ensign
SS-Obersturmführer (SS-Ostuf)	Oberleutnant	Lieutenant
SS-Hauptsturmführer (SS-Hstuf)	Hauptmann	Captain
COMMANDERS		
SS-Sturmbannführer (SS-Stubaf)	Mayor	Commander
SS-Obersturmbannführer (SS-Ostubaf)	Oberstleutnant	Lieutenant Colonel
SS-Standartenführer (SS-Staf)	Oberst	Colonel
SS-Oberführer (SS-Obf)		No equivalence
GENERALS		
SS-Brigadeführer and Major General of the Waffen SS (SS-Brif)	Major General	Brigadier General
SS-Grupenführer and General Lieutenant of the Waffen SS (SS-Gruf)	Generalleutnant	Lieutenant General
SS-Obergruppenführer and General of the Waffen SS (SS-Ogruf)	General of Infantry, Kavallerie.	Lieutenant General
SS-Oberstgruppenführer and Colonel General of the Waffen SS (SS-Obgruf)	General	Captain General
	Generalfeldmarschall	Marshal
SS-Reichsführer SS[2]		No equivalence

1 Some ranks are not directly equivalent to the current Spanish Army ranks.
2 This rank was exclusive to Heinrich Himmler.

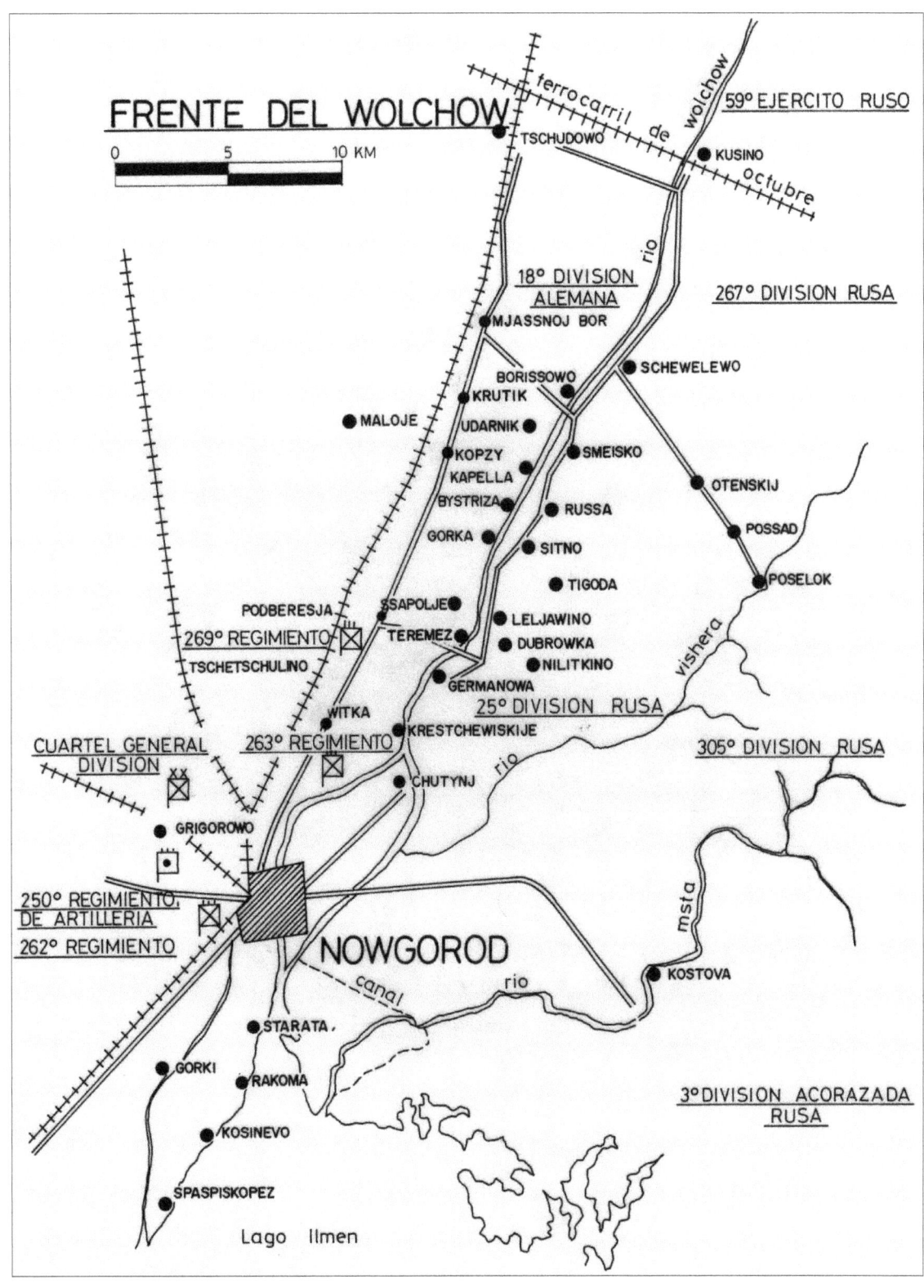

▲ Volkhov Front in January 1942 (NEG).

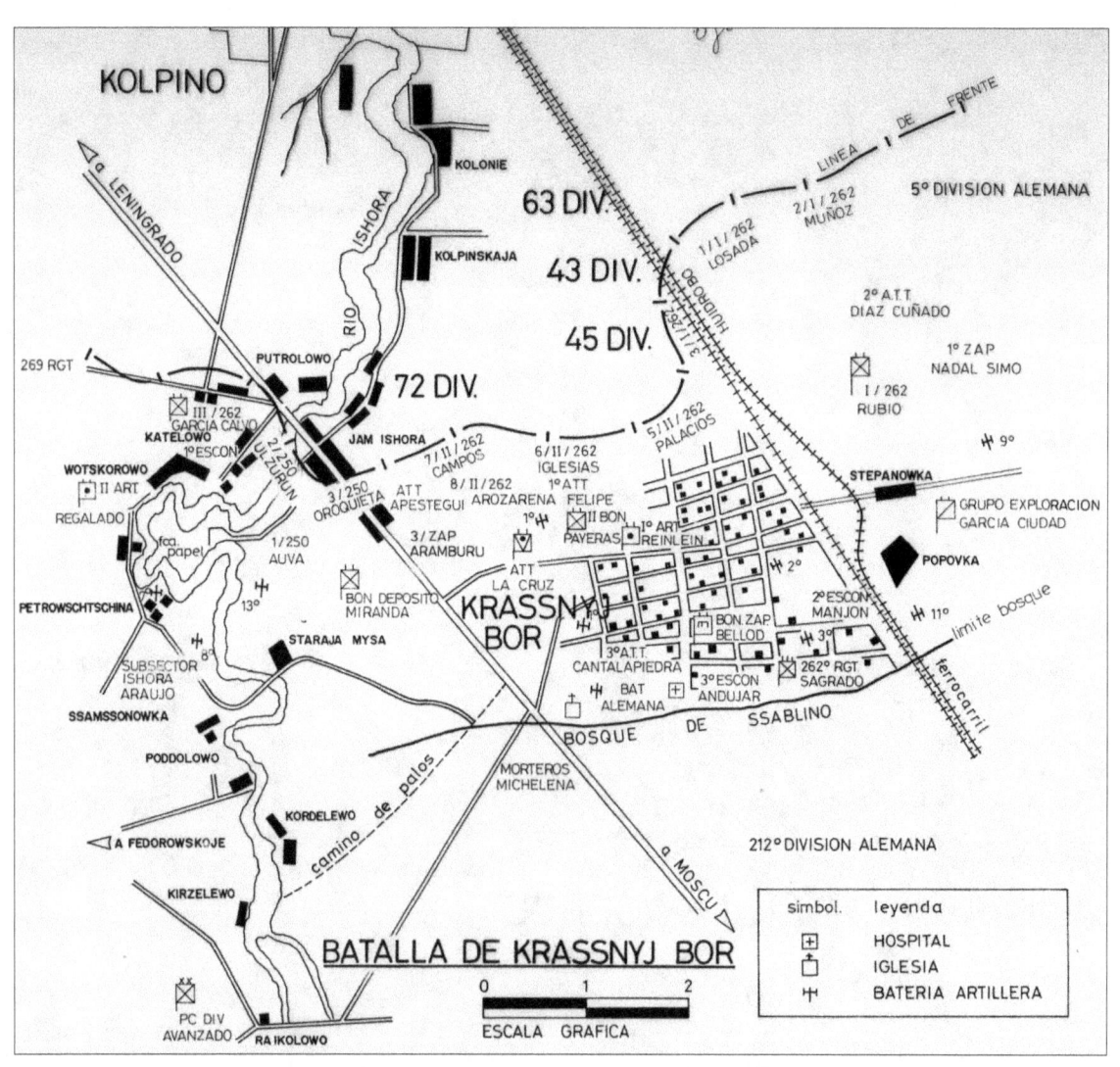
▲ Battle of Krasny Bor in February 1943 (NEG).

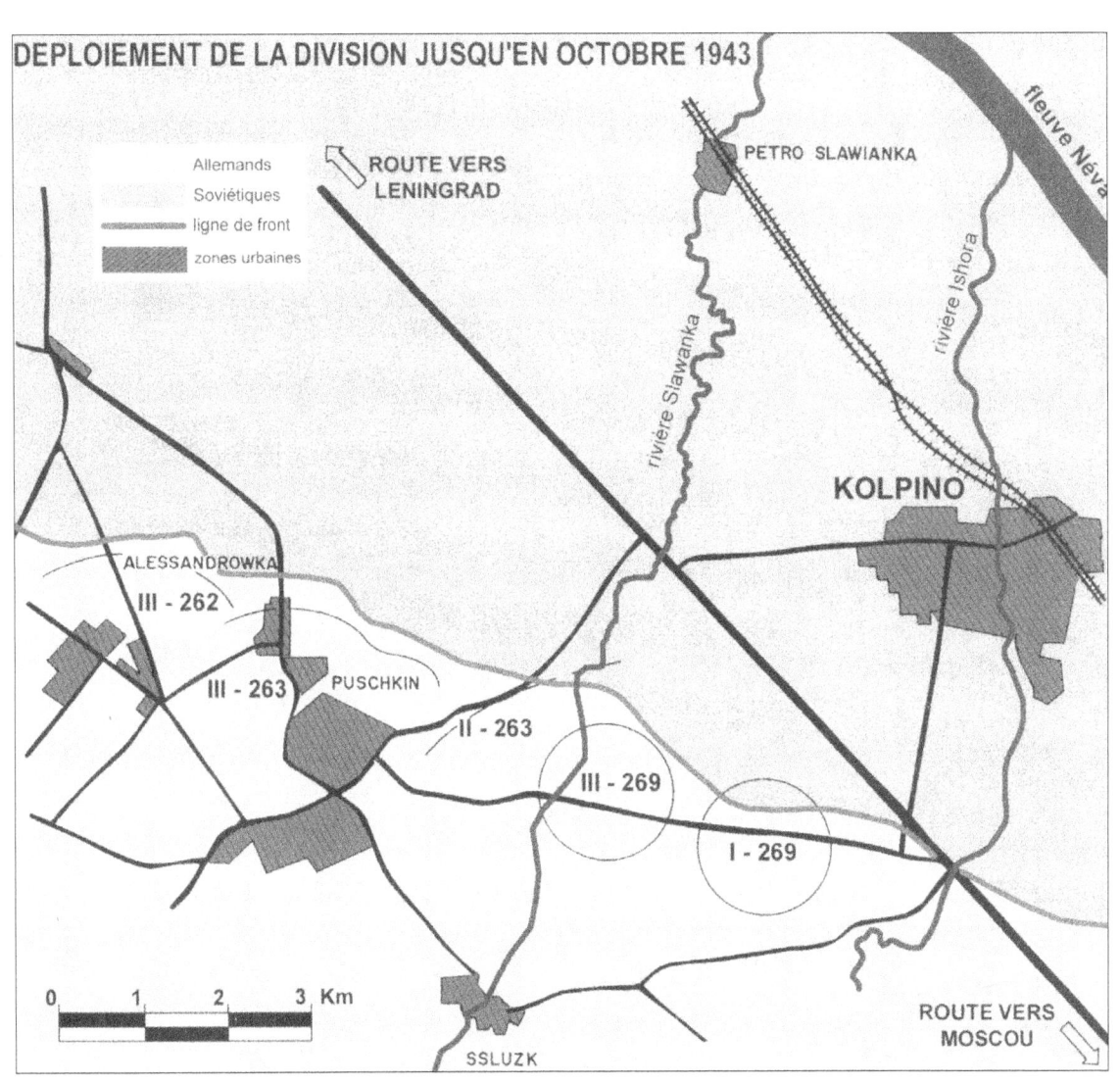

▲ Deployment of the Blue Division in the Kolpino area in October 1943 (JAC).

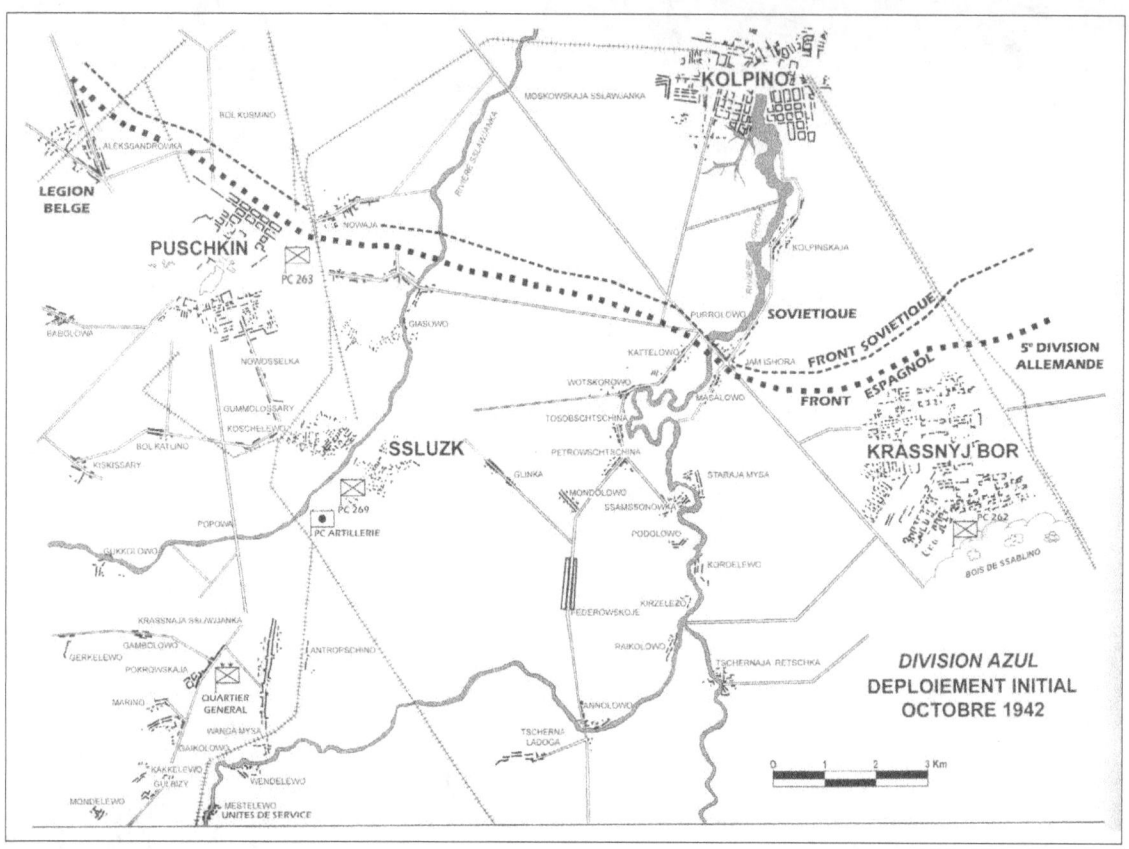

▲ Initial deployment of the Blue Division in the Krasny Bor and Kolpino area in October 1942 (JAC).

▼ Deployment of the Blue Division in the Oraniembaum pocket in October 1943 (JAC).

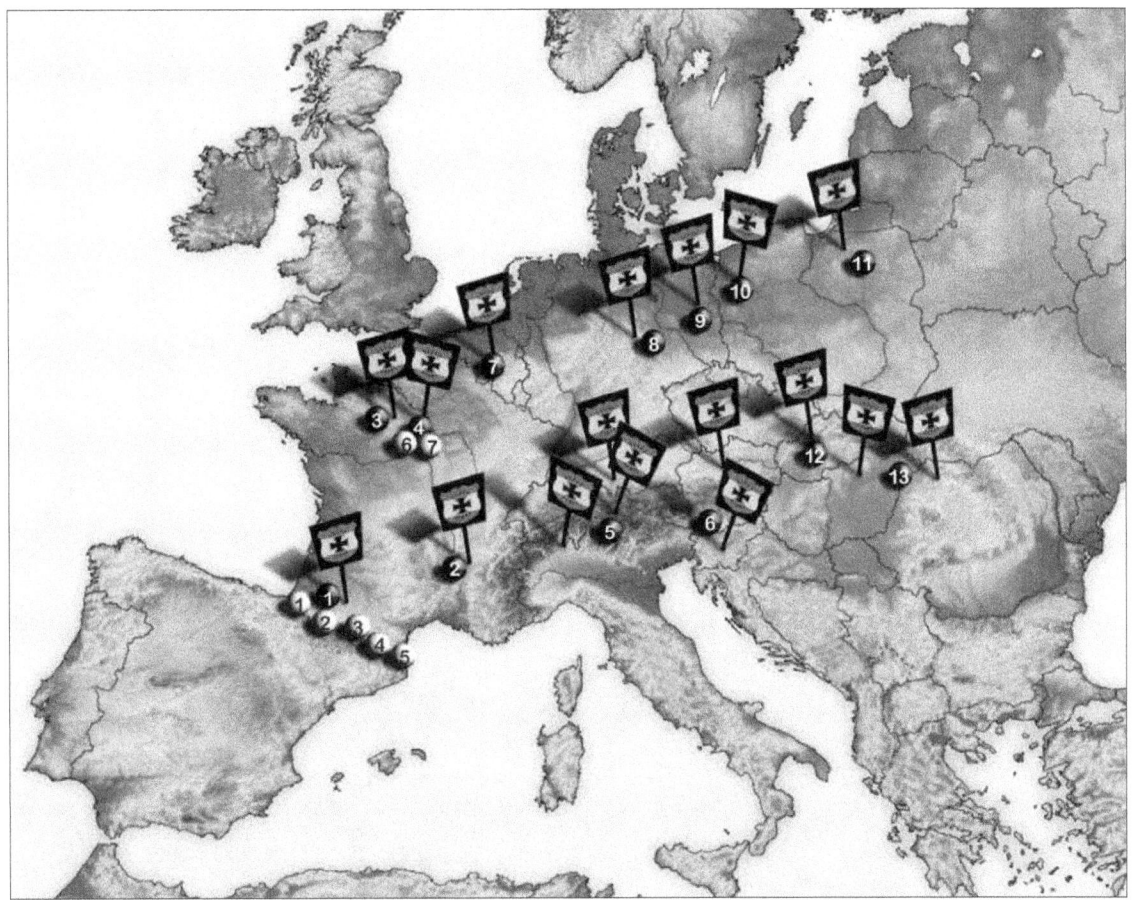

▲ This map shows with white spheres the different locations related to the 'recruitment' of Spaniards crossing the Pyrenean border to enlist in the German army.

1: Hendaye.
2: Andorra.
3: Puigcerd. border.
4: Port Bou.
5: Versailles.
6: Paris.
7: Lourdes.

Marked with black spheres are the various locations. in Europe where Spanish soldiers fought under the LEV banner, both in the Wehrmacht and the Waffen SS.

1. French Pyrenees area. Anti-partisan struggle.
2. French Pre-Alpine area. Anti-Partisan struggle.
3. Landing in Normandy.
4. Queen's Barracks. Versailles.
5. Northern Italy. Anti-partisan struggle.
6. Northern Yugoslavia. Anti-partisan struggle.
7. Belgium. Battle of the Bulge.
8. Battle of Berlin.
9. Defence of the Oder river area.
10. Various clashes. Eastern Front.
11. Various clashes. Eastern front.
12. Training in various Austrian locations.
13. Fighting in Romania and Slovakia.

Courtesy of Almena.

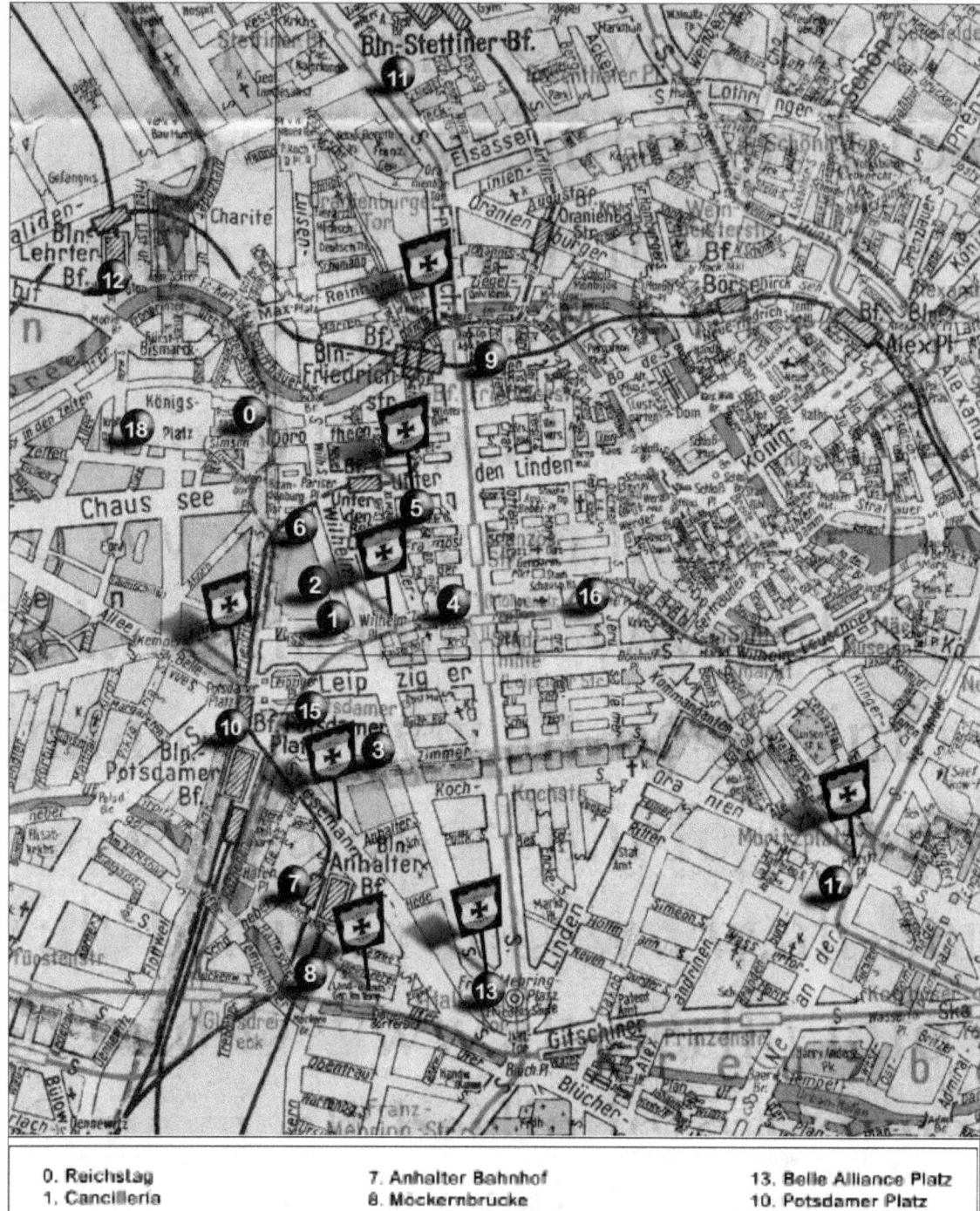

0. Reichstag
1. Cancillería
2. Führerbunker
3. Ministerio del Aire
4. Hotel Kaiserhof
5. Reichsbank
6. Hotel Adlon
7. Anhalter Bahnhof
8. Möckernbrucke
9. Bahnhof Friedrichstrasse
10. Postdamer Bahnhof
11. Stettiner Bahnhof
12. Lehrter Bahnhof
13. Belle Alliance Platz
10. Potsdamer Platz
15. Leipziger Platz
16. Hans Vogtel Platz
17. Moritz Platz
18. Königs Platz

▲ Map of central Berlin in 1945 with the location of the main streets, buildings and places where the Spanish volunteers fought. All these places are mentioned throughout the book. Courtesy of Almena.

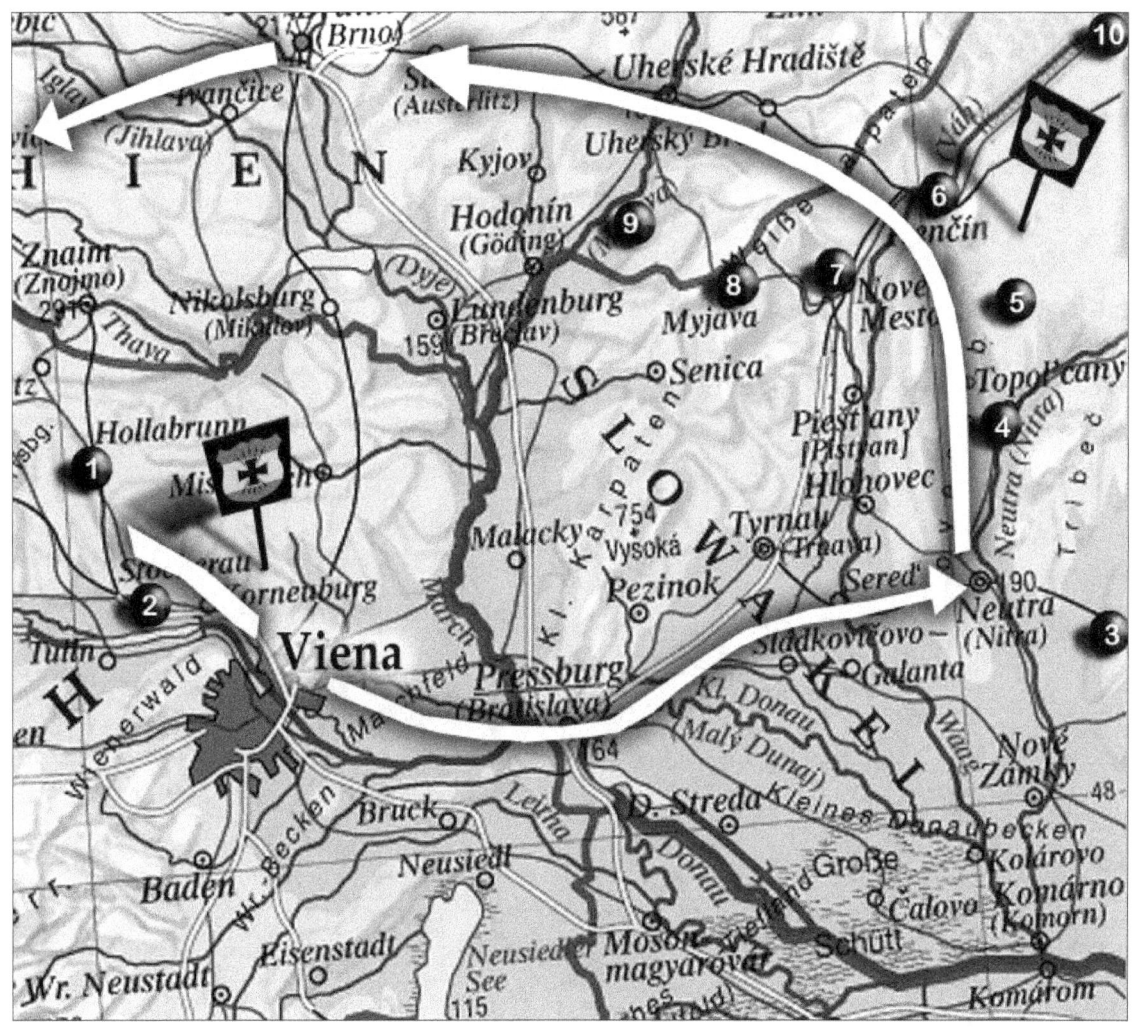

▲ The route followed by the 357. Wehrmacht Infantry Division from the departure from the barracks in Austria to the Slovakian territory (hypothetically up to Nitra) and the subsequent combat retreat in the face of the advance of the Soviet army from Nitra to Ceska Budejovice (in the east) via Brno (February and May 1945).
Locations in the Austrian-Slovak area north-west and north-east of Vienna through which the men of the 102. Spanish Company passed through while being integrated into the 357. Infantry Division.

1 Hollabrun;
2 Stockerau;
3 Vráble;
4 Topoľcany;
5 Bánkovce;
6 Trencín;
7 Nove Mesto na Váhom;
8 Myjava;
9 Stráznice;
10 Belusa.

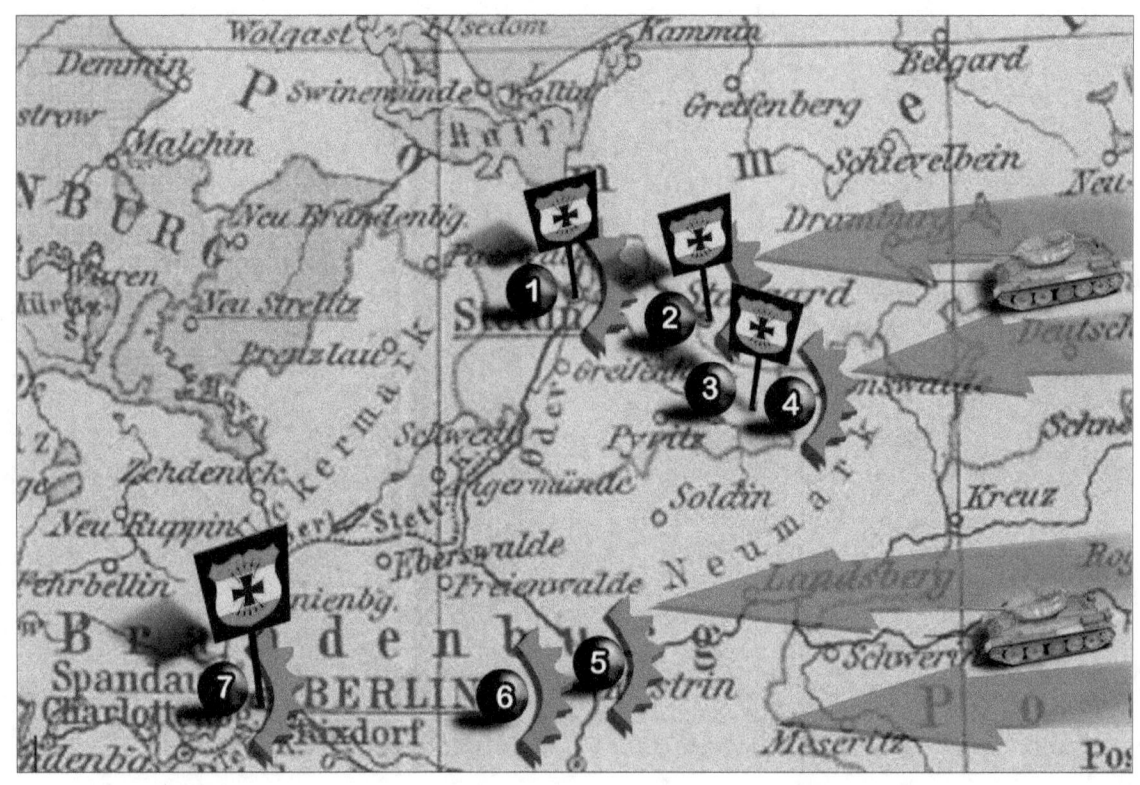

▲ Location of the different locations north and east of Berlin where important battles with Soviet troops took place in 1945: 1 Stettin, 2 Stargard, 3 Kollin, 4 Arnswalde, 5 Kustrin, 6 Seelow, 7 Berlin. In 1, 2 and 3 there were Spanish troops incorporated into the 'Wallonien' Division; and in 7 with Unit. Ezquerra incorporated into the "Nordland" Division.

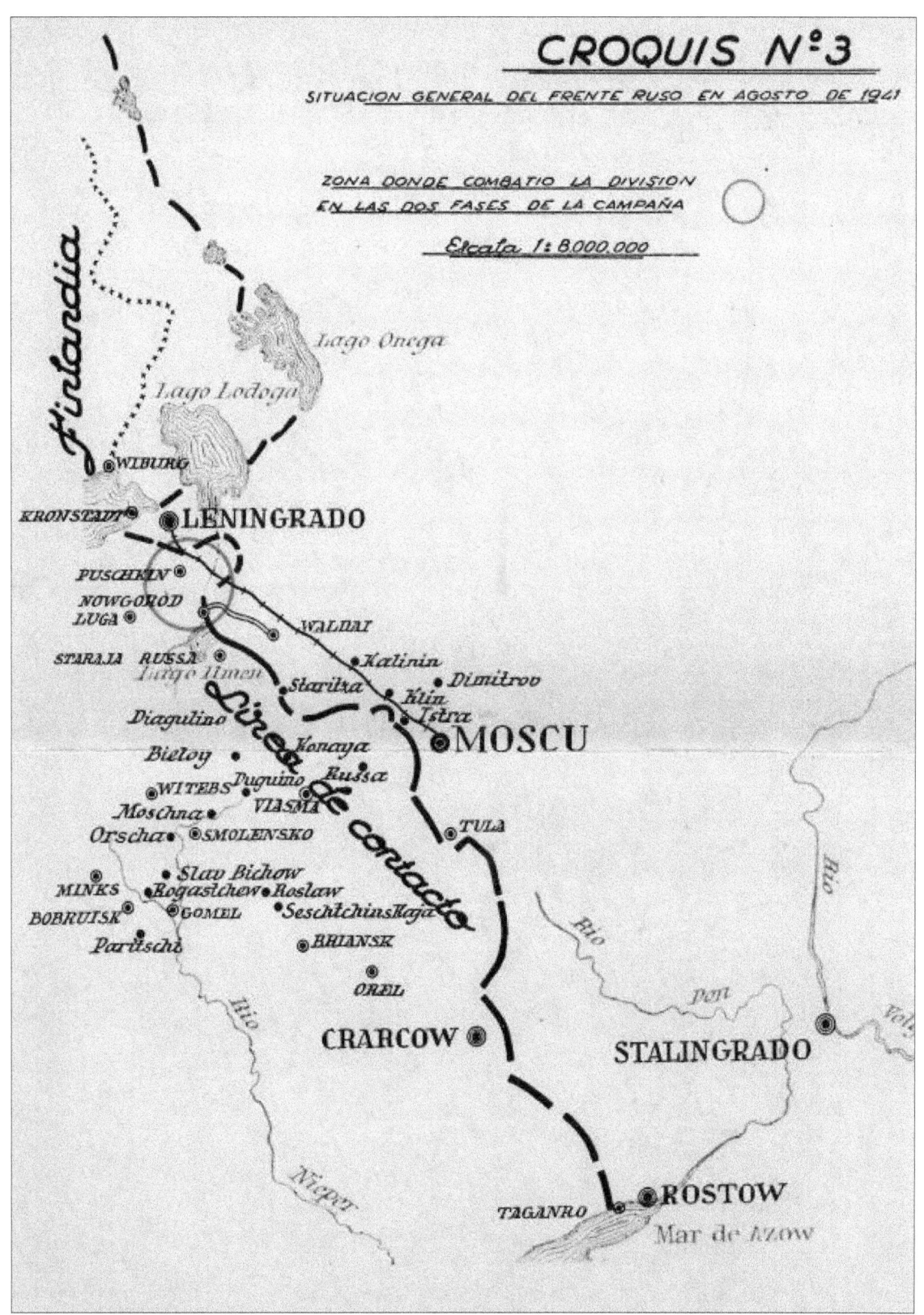

▲ General situation on the Eastern Front in August 1941. Courtesy of the Librería del Guripa.

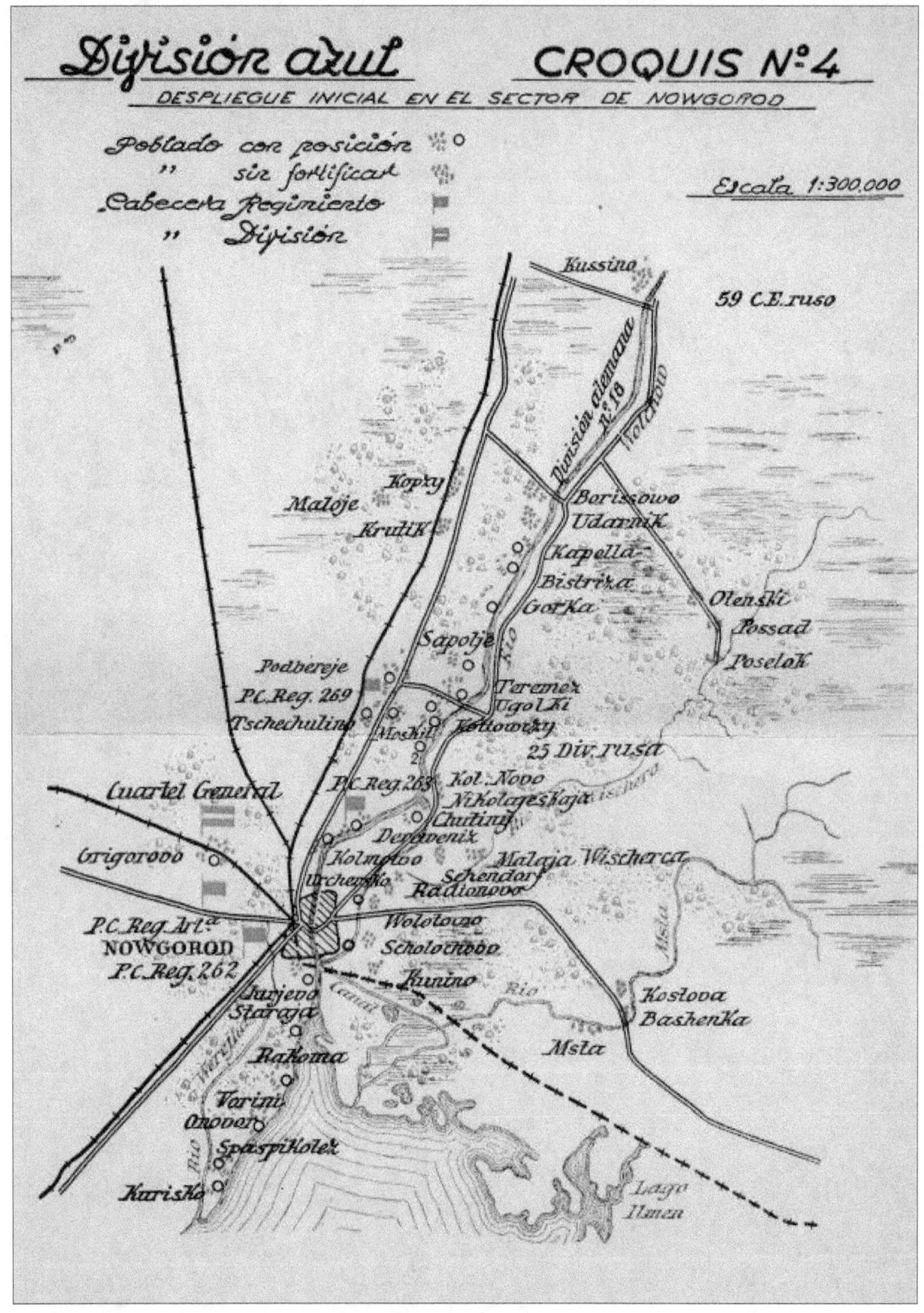

▲ Initial deployment in the Novgorow sector of the Blue Division. Courtesy of the Librería del Guripa.

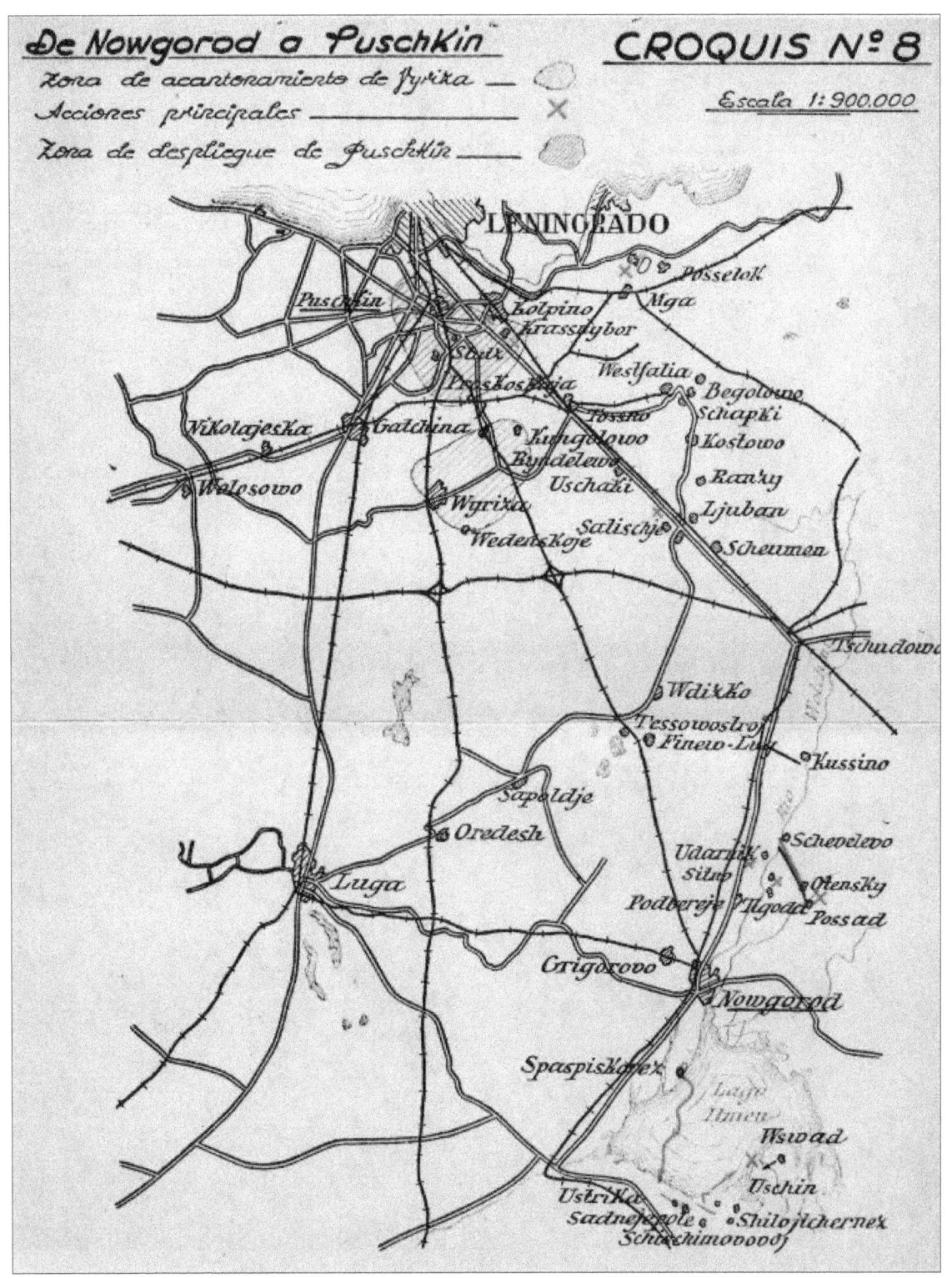

▲ Deployment of the Blue Division from Novgorow to Puschkin, cloning the main actions of the Spanish soldiers. Courtesy of the Librería del Guripa.

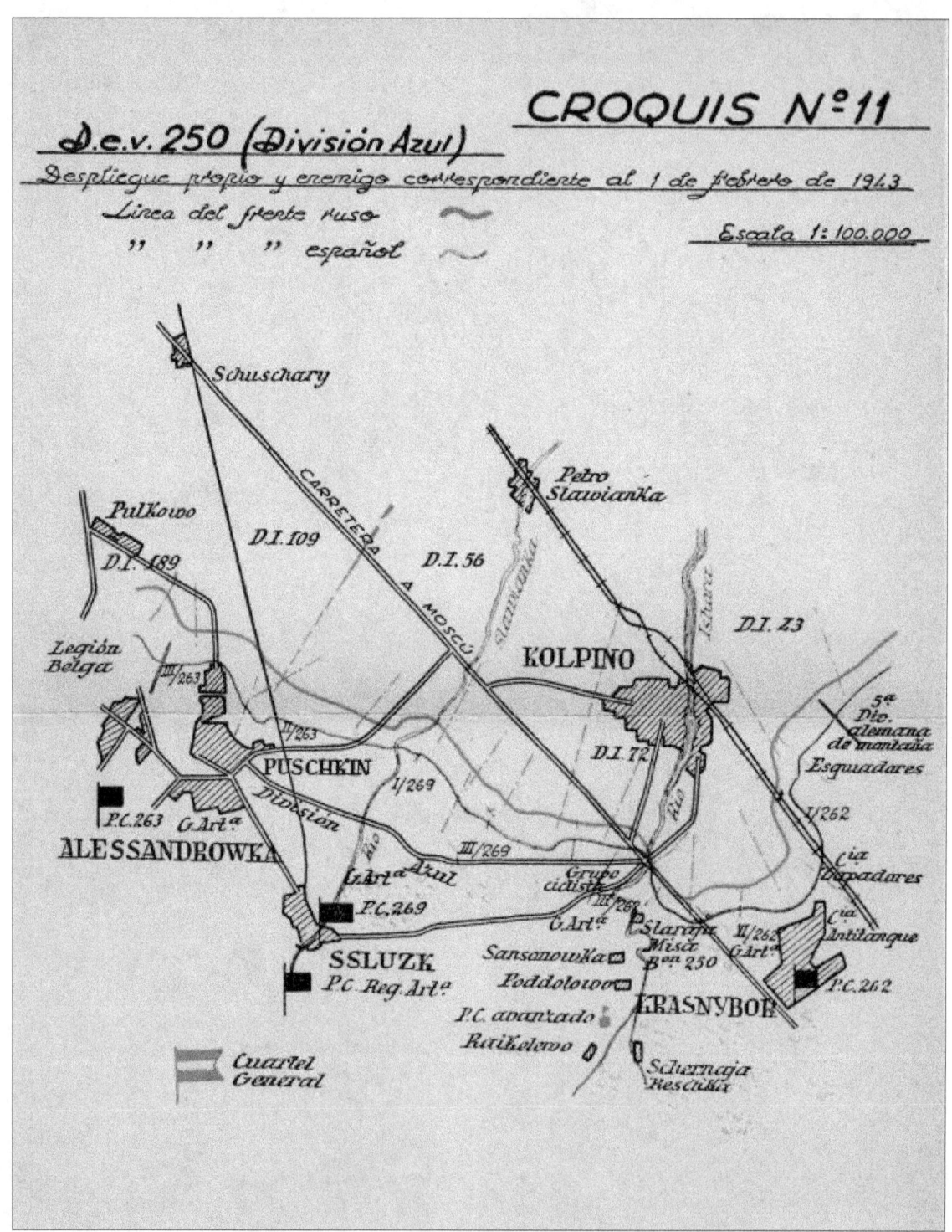

▲ Deployment of the Blue Division on 1 February 1943, days before the Battle of Krasny Bor. Courtesy of the Librería del Guripa.

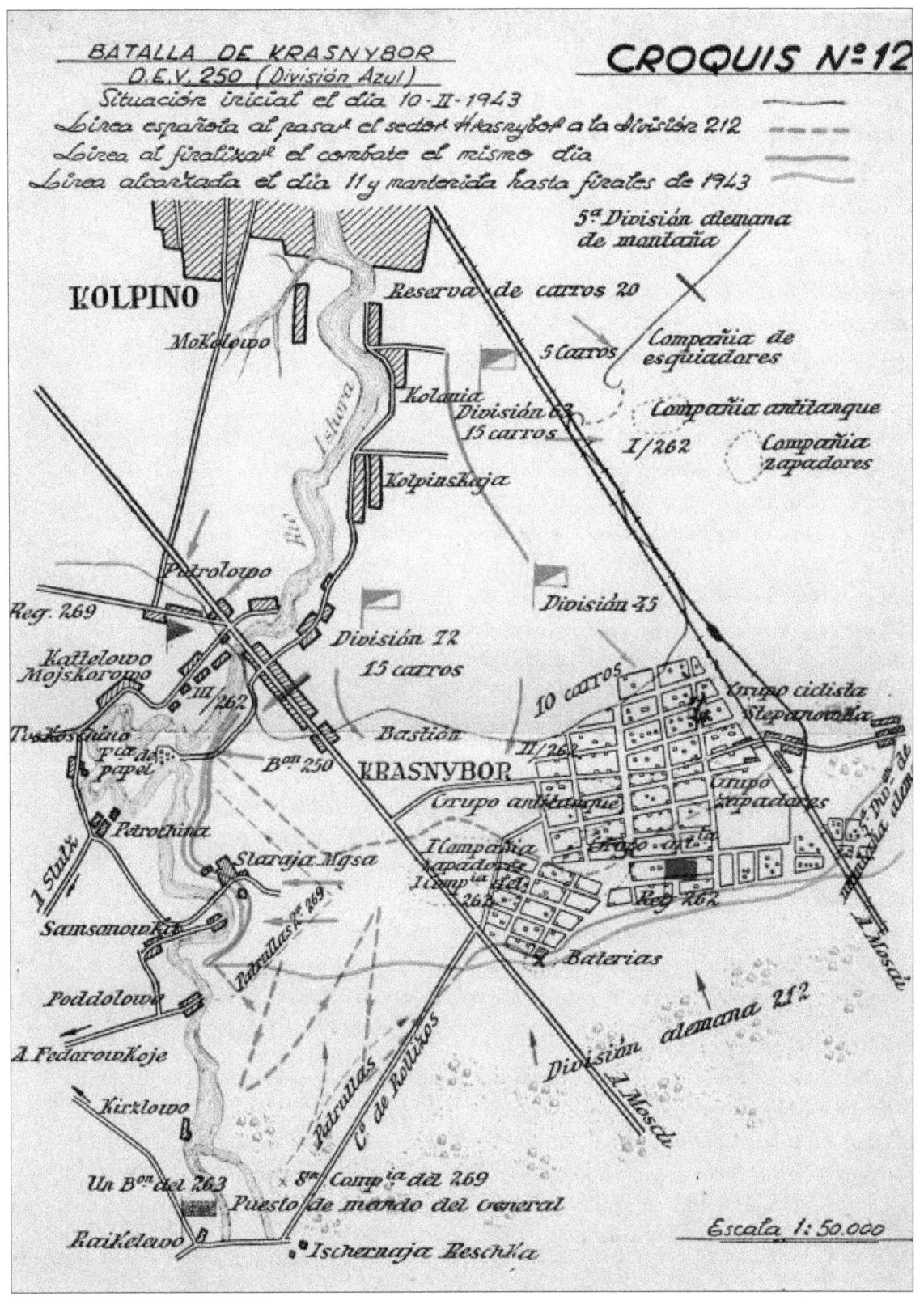

▲ Battle of Krasny Bor (10 February 1943). Courtesy of the Librería del Guripa.

BIBLIOGRAPHY

Ailsby, C. Hell on the eastern front. The Waffen SS war in Russia. 1941-1945. Brown Packaging Books Ltd. 1998.

Alcaide, J. A. Berlín a muerte. Revista española de historia militar. Nº 10. Quirón Ediciones. 2001.

Antill, P. Berlin 1945. End of the thousand year Reich. Osprey Publishing. 2005.

Archivos del Ministerio de Asuntos Exteriores.

Arráez Cerdá, J. Les espagnols de la Wehrmacht. La División Azul. Ciel de Guerre 19. 2011.

Bajo las banderas del III Reich alemán. Españoles en Rusia, 1941-1945. Defensa. Mayo 1999.

Beevor, A. Berlín 1945. La caída. Memoria Crítica. 2002.

Berlin 1945. Magazine 39-45. nº 82. Hors-Série Historica. 2005.

Berlin 1945. Magazine 39-45. nº 83. Hors-Série Historica. 2005.

Biddiscombe, P. Los últimos nazis. El movimiento de resistencia alemán 1944-1947. Books4pocket 74. Inédita Ediciones. 2008.

Bishop, C. Hitler´s foreign divisions. Foreing volunteers in the Waffen-SS 1940-1945. Amber Books Ltd. 2005.

Bowen, Wayne H.: «The Ghost Battalion: Spaniards in the Waffen-SS, 1944-1945», The Historian, vol. 63 (2001).

Boyle D. La II guerra mundial en imágenes. EDIMAT Libros S.A. 2000.

Bueno, J. M. La división y la escuadrilla azul. Su organización y sus uniformes. Aldaba militaria. 2003.

Caballero, C. División Azul. Estructura de una fuerza de combate. Galland Books. 2009.

Caballero, C. Carlomagno. Voluntarios franceses en la Waffen SS. García Hispán. 2003.

Caballero, C. División Azul. Estructuira de una Fuerza de Combate. Galland Books. 2009.

Caballero, C. La División Azul. La Esfera de los Libros. 2019.

Caballero, C; Guillén, S: Las escuadrillas azules en Rusia, Almena, Madrid, 1999.

Caballero, C. Morir en Rusia. La División Azul en la batalla de Krasny Bor. Quirón Ediciones. 2004.

Caballero, C: El batallón fantasma. Españoles en la Wehrmacht y Waffen-SS, 1944-45, CEHRE y ACTV, Alicante-Valencia, 1987.

Caballero, C: Los últimos de los últimos. El batallón fantasma. Extra nº 53. Revista Defensa.

Caballero, C: Waffen-SS. Los centuriones del III Reich. Extra nº 21. Revista Defensa.

Cardona. G. El gigante descalzo. Aguilar. 2003.

Darman, P. Uniforms of world war II. Blitz Editions. 1998.

Davis, B. L. German army. Uniforms and insigniia. 1933-1945. Brockhamptom Press. 1992.

De Caixal, D. Waffen SS. Los templarios de Hitler en combate. Almena. 2003.

Escuadra, A: Bajo las banderas de la Kriegsmarine. Marinos españoles en la Armada alemana, Fundación Don Rodrigo, Madrid, 1998.

Ezquerra, M. Berlín a vida o muerte. García Hispán. 1999.

Fernández, F. Carros de combate y vehículos acorazados alemanes. Servicio de publicaciones del EME. 1988.

Fey, W. Armor battles of the Waffen SS. 1943-45. Stackpole Books. 2003.

García, A M. "Galubaya Divisia". Crónica de la División Azul. Fondo de Estudios Sociales. 2001.

García, M. Semíramis, 1954: El regreso de los cautivos de la División Azul. Nº 46 Revista Española de Historia Militar.

Gil Martínez, Eduardo Manuel. Españoles en las SS y la Wehrmacht. La unidad Ezquerra en la batalla de Berlín 1945. Almena. 2011.

Gómez, M S; Sacristán, E. España y Portugal durante la Segunda Guerra Mundial. Espacio, Tiempo y Forma. Serie V. Hª. Contemporánea, nº 2, 1989, págs 209-225.

Gómez, M S. España y Portugal ante la Segunda Guerra Mundial desde 1939 hasta 1942. Espacio, Tiempo y Forma. Serie V. Hª. Contemporánea, t 7, 1994, págs 165-179.

González Pinilla, A. La División Azul en el periódico Enlace. Gutiskland. 2018.

González Pinilla, A. La Legión Clandestina. Gutiskland. 2021.

Hamilton, A.S. Bloody Street. The Soviet assault on Berlin. Helion. 2020.

Heiber, H. Hitler y sus generales. Memoria crítica. 2005.

Holzträger, H. In a raging inferno. Combat units of the Hitler Youth 1944-45. Helion. 2000.

Jacobsen, HA. Dollinger, H. La Segunda Guerra Mundial. Volumen octavo. Plaza & Janés Editores S.A. 1989.

Keegan, J. Waffen SS. Los soldados del asfalto. Editorial San Martín. 1979.

Kent, C; Wolber, T; Hewitt, C. The Lion and the Eagle: German-Spanish Relations Over the Centuries ; an Interdisciplinary Approach. Berghahn Books, 1999.

Kleinfeld, G. Tambs, L. La división española de Hitler. La División Azul en Rusia. Editorial San Martín. 1983.

Kurowski, F. Hitler´s last bastion. The final battles for the Reich. 1944-1945. Schiffer Military History. 1998.

L´agonie du III. Reich. 1945. Berlin. Batailles & Blindés Hors-Serie nº 1. 2005.

Lagarde, J. German soldiers of world war two. Histoire & Collection. 2005.

La Segunda Guerra Mundial. Victoria en Europa I. Time Life Folio. 1995.

Lehmann, A. En el bunker de Hitler. Testimonio de un niño soldado que vivió los últimos días del Führer. Editorial El Ateneo. 2005.

Loringhoven, B. F. En el bunker con Hitler. Booket. 2007.

Lumsden, R. SS Regalia. Grange books. 1995.

Mabire, J. Los Waffen SS franceses. Los últimos defensores de Hitler. Biblioteca Nacionalsocialista Iberoamericana Volumen V. 2003.

Martínez Canales, F. Lenigrado 1941-44. Almena. 2009.

Mitcham, S W. German order of battle. Volume two. Stackpole Military History Series. 2007.

Mollo, A. The armed forces of World War II. Uniforms, insignia & organization. Greenwich Editions. 2000.

Morales, G; Togores, L E. Las fotografías de una historia. La División Azul. La Esfera de los Libros. 2008.

Moreno, X. Legión Azul y Segunda Guerra Mundial. Actas Editorial. 2014.

Moreno, X. La División Azul. Sangre española en Rusia, 1941-1945. Booket. 2006.

Muñoz, A. Göring´s Grenadiers. The Luftwaffe Field Divisions 1942-1945. Axis Europa Books. 2002.

Nart, J. El Jefe español de las SS. Interviú núm. 339, Madrid, noviembre de 1982.

Norling, S E. Guerreros de Borgoña. Historia de los voluntarios valones de León Degrelle en el Frente del Este. El ocaso de los Dioses (1944-1945). García Hispán Editor. 2008.

Norling, S E. Raza de Vikingos. La División SS Nordland (1943-1945). García Hispán Editor. Segunda Edición.

Norling, S E. The story of a Spanish Waffen SS-Officer. SS-Obersturmführer R. Luis García Valdajos. Siegrunen 79.

Núñez Seixas, X M: «¿Un nazismo colaboracionista español? Martín de Arrizubieta, Wilhelm Faupel y los últimos de Berlín (1944-45)», Historia Social, 51 (2005).

Pallud, JP. Parker, D. Volstad, R. Ardenas 1944: Peiper y Skorzeny. Ediciones del Prado. 1994.

Pérez, C A. Españoles en la Segunda Guerra Mundial (I) Combatiendo por el III Reich. 2006 (texto en internet).

Pérez, Manuel; Prieto, Antonio. Legión Española de Voluntarios en Rusia. Los últimos de la División Azul. Actas Editorial. 2014.

Peterson, D. Waffen SS Camouflage Uniforms & Post-War Derivates. Windrow & Green Ltd 1995.

Puente, M. Yo, muerto en Rusia. Memorias del Alférez Ocañas de la División Azul. Editorial San Martín. 2003.

Recio, R. Españoles en la segunda guera mundial (el frente del este). Vandalia. 1999.

Recio, R. González, A. Uniformes del ejército de tierra alemán. Heer 1933-1945. Euro Uniformes.

Recio, R; González, A. Das Heer. Uniformes y distintivos. Agualarga. 1996.

Ryan, C. La última batalla. La caída de Berlín y la derrota del nazismo. Salvat.2003.

Simons, G. La Segunda Guerra Mundial. Victoria en Europa I. Time Life Folio.1995.

Sourd, Jean-Pierre. True Believers. Spanish Volunteers in the Heer and Waffen-SS, 1944-1945, Europa Books, New York, 2004.

Sourd, Jean-Pierre. Croisés d´un idéal. Dualpha. 2007.

Torres Gallego, Gregorio. El gran libro de Diccionario del Tercer Reich. Tikal. 2009.

Torres Gallego, Gregorio. «Españoles en las Waffen SS. Italia, 1945», Revista Española de Historia Militar, n°10. 2001.

Trevor, H. R. Los últimos días de Hitler. José Janés Editor. 1949.

Tusell, J. Gran Crónica de la Segunda Guerra Mundial. Volumen 16. Edilibro. 1945.

Vadillo, F. Los irreductibles. García Hispán. 1993.

Waffen SS. Los centuriones del Reich. Defensa. Febrero 1993.

Westwell, I. Brandenburgers. The Third Reich´s special forces. Ian Allan Publishing. 2003.

Williamson, G. Las SS: Instrumento de terror de Hitler. Ágata. 2002.

Williamson, G; Andrew, S. The Waffen-SS (4). 24 to 38 Divisions & Volunteer Legions. Osprey Publishing. 2004.

Ziemke, E. F. La batalla de Berlín. Fin del Tercer Reich. San Martín. 1982.

WEBSITES

web www.agrupacion1seis.com

web http://er.users.netlink.co.uk/biblio/ibarruri/armando.htm Política exterior franquista y la Segunda Guerra Mundial por Armando López Salinas

web www.exordio.com

web www.forosegundaguerra.com

web http://greyfalcon.us

web http: //groups.msn.com/memoriadivisionazul/general.msn

web www.gutenberg-e.org

web www.hispanismo.org

web www.history.navy.mil/library/online/germandefberl.htm

web www.historynet.com

web HistoriasigloXX.org

web www.lssah.es

web http://memoriablau.foros.ws

web www.militar.org.ua

web www.mundosgm.com Forum.

web http://www.theeasternfront.co.uk

web usuarios.lycos.es/jnroldan/index.htm

web http://visantain.iespana.es/

web http://wikanda.cordobapedia.es

web Wikipedia. Varios artículos.

web www.ww2f.com

web www.zweiterweltkrieg.org Forum.

TITOLI GIÀ PUBBLICATI - TITLES ALREADY PUBLISHING

www.ingramcontent.com/pod-product-compliance
Lightning Source LLC
LaVergne TN
LVHW081452060526
838201LV00050BA/1775